PETER DONALDSON'S
ILLUSTRATED ECONOMICS

Acknowledgment is due to the following for permission to reproduce illustrations:

BARCLAYS BANK LTD. symbol, page 19;
BRITISH RAILWAYS BOARD symbol,
page 91; CAMERA PRESS Barbara Castle
(photo Colin Davey), page 31, Tom Jones
(photo Terry O'Neill), page 81, Sir Keith
Joseph (photo OBS), page 106, Tony Benn
(photo Jon Blau), page 107; KEYSTONE
PRESS AGENCY Ted Heath, Len Murray,
both page 31, Dennis Healey, page 60;

LLOYDS BANK LTD. symbol, page 19;
MIDLAND BANK LTD. symbol, page 19;
MUSEE DE LOUVRE *Bathsheba* by
Rembrandt, page 81; NATIONAL
WESTMINSTER BANK LTD. symbol, page
19; REX FEATURES Harold Wilson, page 9;
VAUXHALL MOTORS LTD. Vauxhall car,
page 97.

PETER DONALDSON'S
ILLUSTRATED ECONOMICS

EDITED BY CHRIS·JELLEY
SUPPLEMENTARY MATERIAL BY ROY MOORE

BRITISH BROADCASTING CORPORATION

THE PROGRAMMES: First broadcast on BBC-1 on
Sundays at 10.35 a.m. beginning January 11th
1976, with a repeat on the following Tuesdays at
2.30 p.m. Rebroadcast in the Autumn of 1976.

The series is produced by Chris Jelley

Published to accompany a series of programmes
prepared in consultation with the BBC
Further Education Advisory Council.

ISBN 0 563 10971 8
© Peter Donaldson and the British Broadcasting Corporation 1975
First published 1975.

Published by the British Broadcasting Corporation
35 Marylebone High Street, London W1M 4AA.

This book is set in Monotype Univers
Printed and bound by Billing & Sons Limited,
Guildford, Surrey.

CONTENTS

Peter Donaldson, the author as well as presenting the television series which the book accompanies, has done a good deal of other broadcasting and is the author of *Guide to the British Economy, Worlds Apart* and *Economics of the Real World*. He is a Tutor at Ruskin College, Oxford.

Roy Moore, who is also at Ruskin College, has provided the supplementary material other than the cartoons. He has himself written widely in the area of economics, statistics and adult education. He is also engaged in Trade Union Research.

Chris Jelley is the producer of the television series and has also been responsible for editing the book. He has been a teacher of Economics.

INTRODUCTION

In their attitude towards economics and the state of the economy, people mostly fall into one of three groups. There are those who Don't Know and Don't Care; there are those who Don't Know but Do Care and would like to have an understanding of what it is all about; and there are the Know-Alls to whom the whole business is very simple and straightforward.

Over the past few years, the number of uncaring Don't-Knows must have greatly diminished. This is not simply because of the constant bombardment from the mass media of information and comment about the economic situation. It is chiefly due to the fact that we have had to face a novel and alarming combination of unprecedented inflation, unemployment at a level not experienced since the war and a threat of falling living standards—all of which affect people very directly and *personally*.

As a result, economic issues have seldom been the subject of such general public discussion as they are today. And the existence of so many Don't-Knows has made it a field-day for the Know-Alls with their various convictions that setting the economy right calls for a punitive dose of mass unemployment, or a government of national talents or a total destruction of the present system in order to make a fresh start. In the midst of ignorance, prejudice becomes the opinion leader.

This book aims at helping the caring Don't-Knows and getting the Know-Alls to look more closely at what they are saying. It is for the non-economist and the economics beginner. But although the material is presented in as simple and palatable a way as possible, it is no good pretending that making sense of economics and what is happening to the economy can be made easy. One of the objects of the book is to show the complexity of economic matters and that there *aren't* any simple solutions to our economic ills.

Peter Donaldson's Illustrated Economics is also the title of a 15-programme BBC television series first broadcast in 1976. Ideally, the book should be read in conjunction with the series since they both have the same structure of topics and are intended to reinforce each other.

However, the book is also meant to stand on its own. It covers ground which should be of interest to any adult audience—the causes and impact of rising prices, why the number out of work rises and falls, whether the balance of payments matters, the roles of private enterprise and the State in the economy, and where *you* fit into the total economic picture.

The main thread of the text is supplemented throughout by illustrative material. This gives the reader a choice of how much detail he wants to take in at first reading—the main text contains the guts of the argument. Each chapter opens with facts and questions to test the reader's knowledge, interest and prejudice about the subject. Archetypal cartoon figures are used to express commonly held views which are then examined in the main text. For those who want to check how far they have understood what they have read, there is a collection of questions and answers at the end of the book.

This book will not make you into an economist. It will not give you a series of clear-cut solutions to Britain's economic problems. But it should enable you to make more sense of what is written and said about the economy—and to form your own judgment. For some, it may be a stepping-stone to a more thorough study of the subject by joining an economics class or simply through further reading.

IS IT WAGES WHICH ARE PUSHING PRICES UP? THE TRUTH IN ECONOMICS IS RARELY AS SIMPLE AS IT SEEMS.

FUELLING INFLATION

On the face of it, Harold Wilson's view that it is wages which push prices up seems unarguable. Do you agree?
IF YOU ANSWER YES, are you sure that you are not oversimplifying?
■ Do wage increases have to be passed on as price increases; can't part of the impact be absorbed by greater efficiency?
■ Does a 20% wage increase *necessarily* cause a 20% price increase—even in industries which use relatively little labour?
■ Are wages even the *major*—let alone the *only*—cause of inflation? Is it greedy British unions which have pushed up the price of oil?
IF YOUR ANSWER IS NO, then how do you account for the following?

■ Wages have risen significantly faster than prices.
■ Wages have also risen faster than any increase in output produced per worker.

Whether you agree with Harold Wilson's view or not depends partly on how sympathetic you are to the unions and how powerful you think they are. But it also depends on the way you see the economics of inflation. We are all affected by inflation—some more than others—and many of us are blamed for actually causing it through our pay increases. In this chapter some of the key facts and relationships are presented which should help to unravel a little of the cat's cradle of inflation.

In 1974:
Wages rose 29%
Prices rose 19%

'One man's wage increase is another man's price increase.'

Do you remember those golden years of the 1950's and the 1960's when we used to worry ourselves sick about annual price rises of 3% or 4%? It's a far cry from our recent concern about whether they can be kept below the 30% mark. We are right to be alarmed by price increases of the order we have had in the past few years because inflation on this scale makes life difficult for all of us: for the housewife desperately trying to make ends meet, for the thrifty trying to find a safe outlet for their savings, for the firm trying to compete in international markets. And there is always the danger that prices will completely take off into hyper-inflation—faster and faster price increases until in the end the value of the currency is totally destroyed.

Something has to be done, and done urgently. But before we can tackle the problem of inflation effectively, we need to know what causes it. Unfortunately, as we shall see in this and the next chapter, there are very different views about just why prices have exploded as they have.

However, for some economists and politicians, there is no doubt about the cause. Inflation is simply the result of paying ourselves too much. The blame is put squarely at the door of trade unions powerful enough to extort wage increases greatly in excess of rises in the cost of living. Companies then have to recoup their soaring costs by raising the prices of their products. The facts certainly seem to support the case. In 1974, for example, prices rose 19%. Wages that year increased by no less than 29%.

Wages and prices

It seems very obvious that wages are the villain of the piece. But the obvious conclusion is not necessarily the right one. Wages rising faster than prices doesn't prove that wages are therefore the whole cause of inflation—which is what we are invited to believe by simply putting the two sets of figures together. To see that matters might be a shade more complex, let's look behind just one of those frightening bills that come through the letterbox. Why has the price of electricity increased so much?

The price of electricity

Apart from dearer food, the mounting cost of keeping warm is one of the main ways in which we are all hit by inflation. About 6% of average family spending is on fuel and lighting. Low income groups spend an even greater proportion on these items, and have therefore been the worst sufferers from the massive rise in fuel prices which has taken place in recent years.

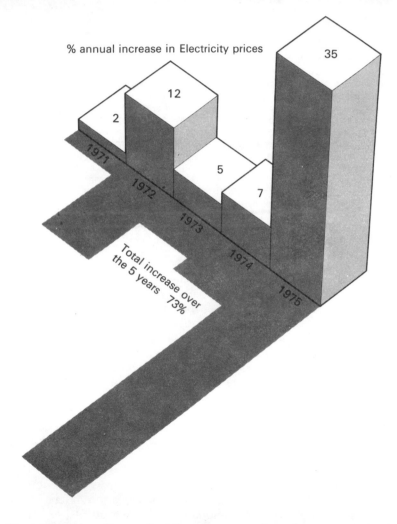

% annual increase in Electricity prices

2 — 1971
12 — 1972
5 — 1973
7 — 1974
35 — 1975

Total increase over the 5 years 73%

IT STANDS TO REASON OF COURSE IT'S THE UNIONS CAUSING INFLATION.

POWER MEN WANT 30%

The Electricity Council says that these increases have been necessary to cover its rising costs and meet the financial target set for it by the government. Since two of its main costs are labour and fuel for the generating stations (of which 95% are coal-fired), need we look any further for the cause of higher electricity charges? Every winter the power workers and the miners threaten to bring the economy to a halt. They are both organised in powerful unions, and not worried about pricing themselves out of work because postwar governments have generally been committed to maintaining full employment. On this view, it is the combination of free collective bargaining and guaranteed full employment which has proved the sure recipe for inflation.

But is it true? *Is* this why you are paying so much more for electricity?

Suppose that your electricity bill comes to £100 a year. Of that £100, nearly half (£44) will go to meeting the cost of the coal and oil needed for the generating stations. £15 will pay for wages and salaries, and about £41 will cover overheads of one kind or another—rents, rates, insurance, depreciation and interest.

Now what happens if, during the coming winter, both the miners and the electricity workers secure outrageously massive wage settlements—rises of no less than 50%? Would you expect your electricity bill also to rise by 50%?

Labour accounts for about half the cost of producing coal. The effect of a 50% wage increase, if it is all passed on, is therefore to raise the price of coal by 25%.

As we have just seen, in the electricity industry, every £100's worth produced is made up of £44 fuel costs plus £15 wages plus £41 other costs. If coal were the only fuel used, then the effect of the miners' rise is that coal bought by the electricity industry for £44 now costs £55; and the 50% settlement for the electricity workers adds a further £7.50 to the previous £16 labour costs.

So the consumer finds that electricity previously costing £100 will now cost £118.50 (and *not* £150). The combined effects of wage rises in both the coal and electricity industries is to increase the price of electricity, not by 50%, but by 18½%.

The anatomy of an electricity bill

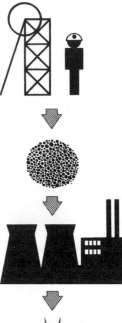

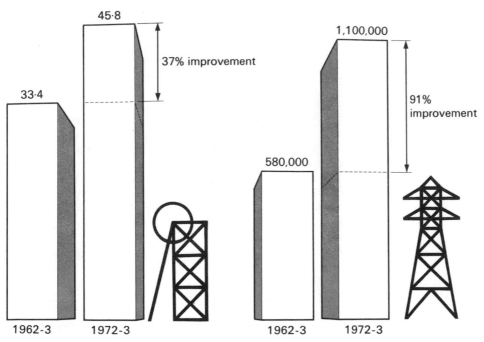

Cwt. of coal per manshift

45·8

37% improvement

33·4

1962-3   1972-3

Units of electricity per employee

1,100,000

91% improvement

580,000

1962-3   1972-3

Nor is this quite the end of the wage story. Prices need not be pushed up even to this extent if at the same time improvements in productivity are taking place. If workers can produce sufficiently more to match their wage rises, then there is no reason why their settlements should be inflationary.

In fact, of course, recent wage rises in the fuel industries have far exceeded productivity increases. But nonetheless, as a result of better working practices, more up-to-date machinery and improved management, productivity *has* risen substantially in both the coal and electricity industries—and contributed towards holding prices down.

Despite all this, wage rises are part of the inflationary process and trade unions do use their strength in vulnerable sectors of the economy to improve the relative position of their members—sometimes at the expense of weaker and less organised groups. But *if* inflation is due mainly to costs pushing up prices, then don't forget that wages are only one of the costs doing the pushing. Also very important in increasing your fuel bill and other prices are rises in the *capital costs* of production, the costs of *imported materials*, and the effect of *government policies*.

■ In an age of rapid technological change, producers find that their plant and machinery becomes obsolescent more and more rapidly. Faced with the mounting cost of renewing them, they may therefore raise prices in order to get hold of the necessary funds.

■ Britain depends heavily on imported raw materials. Between 1970 and 1974 the price of imported materials rose on average by 108% and oil prices more than quadrupled. There were a number of reasons for this upsurge but two stand out as particularly important. Firstly, most of the industrial countries were booming at that time and demanding raw materials faster than they could be produced. Secondly, the poorer commodity producing countries were flexing their muscles and trying to squeeze a better deal from the rich consuming countries. And, in the case of Britain, a further upward twist to import prices came from the falling overseas value of the pound (*discussed in detail in Chapter 7*).

■ In two ways, governments can themselves fuel inflation. They can raise taxes like petrol duty or VAT which directly increase prices. Or they can indirectly push up prices by opting for deflationary policies which aim at cutting down the level of spending in the economy. In this situation, firms have to spread their expensive overheads over a smaller volume of sales—and try to cover their higher unit costs by raising prices.

We know that costs have risen and that prices have risen. What we *don't* know is what caused what to rise. Have wage increases, for example, just been defensive responses to other costs rising, or have they been the prime cause of inflation? What has been said so far suggests that they can hardly have been the only cause—and perhaps have not even been the main one. But that is not to deny that the prospects for bringing inflation under control are threatened by wage demands based on expectations that inflation is going to get worse. If we all try not just to compensate ourselves for past price increases but also to protect ourselves against what we fear are going to be still faster price rises in the future—then the danger is that we shall prove ourselves right.

Tackling cost inflation means breaking into a number of vicious circles.

Higher import costs, for example, push up prices. If we then try to maintain our living standards by getting equivalent wage rises, prices increase still further. But that in turn weakens the value of the pound and raises import prices once again.

Similarly, putting direct controls on the prices firms can charge may weaken

PRICES

Wage costs

Import costs

Government costs

Capital costs

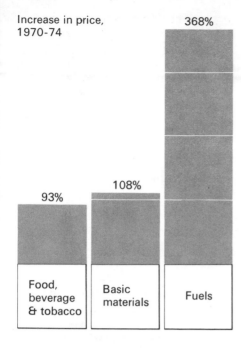

Increase in price, 1970-74

93% — Food, beverage & tobacco
108% — Basic materials
368% — Fuels

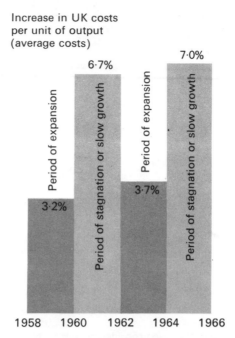

Increase in UK costs per unit of output (average costs)

3·2% — 1958 — Period of expansion
6·7% — 1960 — Period of stagnation or slow growth
3·7% — 1962 — Period of expansion
7·0% — 1964 — Period of stagnation or slow growth

1958   1960   1962   1964   1966

HOW THE PRICES OF OUR IMPORTED MATERIALS HAVE RISEN

The biggest increase of all has, of course, been in the price of oil. In August 1973 (before the Middle East War) the over-all cost of crude oil to a British company was 2 dollars a barrel. By May 1975 it had risen to over 10 dollars a barrel, a fivefold increase in less than two years.

HOW LOW GROWTH CAN PUSH UP COSTS AND PRICES

When the economy is expanding, if costs increase they can be spread over a greater volume of output, so that average costs—and therefore prices—need not rise so fast. Slow or zero growth on the other hand means more cost pressure.

their incentive to invest in new plant and machinery. Less investment means smaller improvements in productivity to absorb the impact of wage rises. And if governments try to limit incomes, they face the danger of a tug-of-war between themselves and the unions. If Chancellors try to grab back what they see as excessive wage increases by raising taxes, then the price rises which *they* cause can stimulate even larger demands in the future.

So what is the answer? That's not easy—but it must lie not in demanding just *wage* restraint, but in a concerted attempt to control *all* the possible cost pressures on prices. Some of the elements in the package which are needed we shall be looking at in later chapters: the need to give people better automatic protection against inflation if they are not to take matters into their own hands, the need to halt the downward drift in the external value of the pound, the need for governments to provide an expansionary climate in which we can all be better off rather than some at the expense of others.

But all that assumes that we *are* suffering from cost inflation. Not everyone agrees. There are some economists who say that it's not the unions, it's not import prices, it's not costs at all which are responsible for rising prices. For them, cost increases are symptoms rather than causes; the real cause of inflation is that there is too much money floating around the economy—allowing individuals and governments to spend beyond their means.

AN INTERNATIONAL COMPARISON

Compare the nature of the U.K.'s inflation— and its causes—in the 'sixties with the performance of her major competitors; would you put the blame for Britain's poor showing more on wage inflation or on lower efficiency?

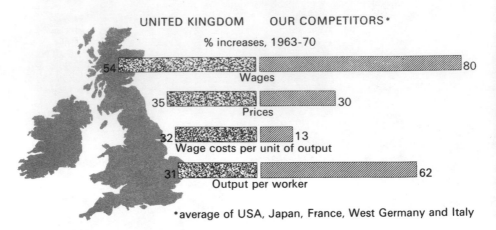

UNITED KINGDOM   OUR COMPETITORS*

% increases, 1963-70

54 / 80 — Wages

35 / 30 — Prices

32 / 13 — Wage costs per unit of output

31 / 62 — Output per worker

*average of USA, Japan, France, West Germany and Italy

Answer:

Wages have risen considerably faster on average in the other countries, but wage costs in relation to output have risen much more here than abroad. This is because output per worker has only increased in the U.K. by half as much as in the other countries. The result is that prices have risen rather faster here.

It can be argued that the most significant factor behind the U.K.'s poor showing is the much slower rise in output per worker, rather than wages rising too fast.

MONEY'S THE PROBLEM

BANK OF ENGLAND

SOME BLAME GOVERNMENTS AND BANKS FOR CAUSING INFLATION BY CREATING *TOO MUCH MONEY.* BUT THEIR CASE IS FAR FROM PROVED.

MONEY SUPPLY
£ million

Inflation is often described as being caused by 'too much money chasing too few goods'. The amount of money in the economy, in the form of notes and coins and current accounts at banks, is known as the *money supply* or *money stock*, and has increased massively in recent years. In 1968 it amounted to £150 per head of the population; by 1974 the figure had risen to £240 per head.

Over the same period the amount of money which the government has wished to borrow for its own needs has grown rapidly, whilst at the same time inflation has really accelerated:

	Government borrowing requirement	Inflation
1968	£1,300 million	6%
1974	£7,600 million	19%

There clearly seems to be a link between all these figures—so do you think the government could bring inflation down by holding back the money supply or by borrowing less itself? This chapter looks at the argument that increases in the money supply are a cause of inflation—and therefore a possible way of dealing with it.

Pocket money, pin money, beer money, housekeeping money. We are always complaining that we don't have enough of it. But is that what we really mean?

Suppose that tomorrow morning we woke up to a world without money— because overnight a plague of money weevils had eaten up every bank note, coin and bank ledger in existence. It would be a world in which we were no poorer. The factories, the farms, the transport system and the shops would still all be there and capable of producing goods and distributing them. It would be a world very much more cumbrous and inconvenient to run because money is an extremely useful invention. But money is not the same thing as wealth.

WEALTH
Wealthy people do not hold very much of their wealth in the form of money. Inland Revenue figures suggest that people with wealth between £100,000 and £200,000 hold less than £3 in every £1,000 in the form of money—their cash at home and their current account at the bank.

By contrast, £620 out of every £1,000 is in the form of stocks and shares, with a further £190 in property. They prefer to earn interest from their wealth to the advantage of liquidity.

MONEY
Which of the following would you class as money?

premium bonds
banknotes and coins
stocks and shares
current account at bank or Giro

Money is anything which is liquid, which means that it can easily be sold at a guaranteed value. So in this sense current accounts as well as notes and coins are money, since cheques can be drawn upon them without giving your bank notice. Premium bonds can only be cashed after a delay, whilst stocks and shares can be sold but not at a guaranteed value.

The other items in the list above do not count as money because either they can't be sold *immediately* or for a *guaranteed* value.

The temptation of easy credit

We all like easy credit. Cheap and plentiful overdrafts, generous hire purchase terms, low building society rates—they all make it possible for us to buy things in advance of earning and saving the means to pay for them. But there is an obvious danger for the weak-willed that the lures of the 'never-never' can lead them into living impossibly beyond their means.

Some economists argue that the same is true of governments. They have financed their activities by increasing the amount of money in the economy. And that is what has caused prices to rise. Certainly the money supply has persistently increased, and it has been paralleled by inflation:

CASE I

In 1844 the Bank Charter Act restricted the quantity of bank notes which the Bank of England could print to the amount of bullion which it held (then about £14 million) plus an additional 'fiduciary issue' of £14 million unbacked by gold. Subsequently, the restriction was removed. One hundred and thirty years later, in 1974, the note issue stood at just under £6000 million. Meanwhile, although it is impossible to make accurate comparisons, prices had enormously increased—perhaps more than six-fold.

CASE II

In 1971 the government made bank and building society lending much easier. In the following two years, the money supply rose by over 28%. Prices during these years began to increase at an unprecedented 10-20%. And house prices nearly doubled.

How banks make money

There certainly seems strong circumstantial evidence that money is at the root of the inflationary evil. But before looking more carefully at the *Monetarist* case, we need firstly to see how the increase in money and credit has come about.

However much we complain about their declining purchasing power and the fact that the promise printed on them is meaningless, we still all quite happily accept banknotes as a means of payment. It is just this general acceptability which makes them (and anything else which is similarly acceptable) be classed as *money*.

But banknotes, like coin, are only part of what economists call 'the money supply'. They have become the small change of the system.

Far more important are bank *deposits* which banks have created greatly in

£4,300 million

There is more than twice as much money held in current bank deposits as in notes and coins in circulation.

£9,400 million

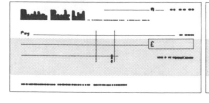

THEY'RE NOT WORTH THE PAPER THEY ARE PRINTED ON.

excess of their holdings of banknotes. In other words, if we all go along to the banks tomorrow and withdraw our deposits, the banks simply won't have enough cash to meet our demands. In fact the whole business of banking depends on us *not* all asking for our money at the same time. It's a gigantic confidence trick. How have they got away with it? How have banks managed to create 'credit money' unbacked by banknotes? The answer looks very different according to whether we approach the question from the viewpoint of an individual bank or that of the banking system as a whole.

An individual bank, say Barclays, will describe its business like this:

One banker's story

'What we do is to attract customers to deposit cash with us—for safekeeping, convenience, and, if they have a deposit account, to earn interest. Every day, we have people coming into our branches and withdrawing cash. But every day, there are others who make fresh deposits of cash. Over a long period of time we have learned that the two by and large cancel each other out, and that we there-fore have to keep only a small proportion of total deposits as banknotes in our tills to meet any excess of withdrawals over new deposits. Rather than leave the rest idle, what we do is to re-lend it to other customers by, for example, granting them overdrafts. Admittedly, in the unlikely event of a mass demand for deposits to be exchanged for cash, we would be temporarily embarrassed. But rest assured. We lend very carefully, and in due course we would be able to call in our loans and meet our customers' requirements in full.'

In other words, the individual banker claims that it is only after *you* have deposited cash that he can lend to others. He's not creating new money—just making what there is work harder.

But the picture of how the banks operate collectively is very different. Suppose that Barclays grants an overdraft to one of its customers who uses it to buy a car. The car dealer takes his £500 and puts it into his own bank account—at National Westminster. To them, it looks like any other fresh deposit of cash. National Westminster have no way of knowing that it is the result of lending by Barclays. But, like Barclays, they know from experience that any £500 of deposits requires only a small proportion of banknotes to be held in their tills. So they, in turn, re-lend the rest. And the customer who consequently gets an overdraft from National Westminster may use it to make a payment to a client of Lloyds—which enables them, after making the appropriate deductions of cash to be kept in their tills, to make further loans. . . .

The whole banking story

So when banks lend, and those loans are then used to make payments, they enable fresh deposits to be created elsewhere in the banking system. Collec-

BANKING SYSTEM

Government   Public
                  confidence

tively, they create 'credit money' (which has no physical existence other than as entries in their ledgers) far in excess of their holdings of notes and coin. But of course there is a limit to the process. They must always be ready to meet any demands for cash which customers are ever likely to make. However, because today (and it wasn't the case in the nineteenth century) we are confident that the banks are not in a state of imminent collapse, we don't keep going to the banks to check that our money is still there. That means that the amount of ready cash that the banks have to hold is relatively tiny—in practice, only about 5% of their total deposits. On top of that, they also have a second line of 'reserve assets' which could be quickly converted into cash if needs be.

Banks are therefore literally manufacturers of money—and that's a profitable business to be in. However much your bank manager may sometimes given an impression to the contrary, banks *want* to lend money. It's no sin in their eyes for you to borrow. They depend on the interest you pay for their living. Left to their own devices, they would be constantly searching for creditworthy customers to whom they could lend.

But they are not left to their own devices. The amount of money they can create mainly depends on governments. It is governments who supply the cash and some of the other reserve assets on which the banks' pyramid of credit is built. It is governments who lay down rules about the reserves which banks (and other lenders) should hold, and it is governments who try to direct or persuade the financial institutions to ease or tighten credit in line with current economic policy.

There are two reasons why the money supply has so enormously expanded over the years. One is technical and nobody argues about it, but the other concerns policy and lies at the heart of the controversy about whether it is too much money which is the cause of inflation.

■ Every Christmas, because we are all spending more than usual, the Bank of England increases the number of banknotes in circulation. It doesn't make us any richer by doing so. It is simply that, if they didn't, there would be an inconvenient shortage of notes—which would have to be got round by the shops giving more credit to their customers and banking their takings more frequently to make the limited note supply circulate more rapidly. In just the same way, in a growing economy, the money supply needs to be expanded year by year to lubricate the increased flow of transactions which take place between firms and individuals.

■ The second reason why the money supply has increased is because governments need finance which they can't, or won't, raise in other ways.

Governments have been spending more than they have collected in taxes. Their consequent 'borrowing requirement' has partly been met by printing and issuing bonds, National Savings Certificates and the like, to the general public; but they have borrowed from the banks as well—who also hold government bonds and Treasury bills (three month loans to the government) which form part of the banks' reserve assets. In other words, government borrowing from the banks has meant that governments have had to sanction a multiple increase in the money supply—which, of course, has suited the banks very well.

Government overspending financed by resort to the printing presses—that's the cause of inflation according to the Monetarists. This group of economists sees the answer to spiralling prices in making governments exercise more self-discipline. The money supply should not be allowed to grow faster than the rate at which output is expanding. It is not difficult to see why governments have been reluctant to follow their advice. None of the three alternatives to financing part of their spending through an increased money supply is very attractive for them.

■ Tax increases are one way in which governments can maintain their spend-

Why has the money supply increased so much?

The Monetarist Solution

18

ing without borrowing from the banks. No government relishes that prospect.

■ Cutting government spending, i.e. reducing their borrowing requirement, seems at first sight a much more politically popular solution—until people realise that it means, not simply the elimination of government extravagance and waste, but a reduction in the range and quality of State services which form part of our standard of living.

■ Restricting bank lending to the private sector is the third possibility. If governments continued to borrow from the banks without the money supply increasing, then it would have to be at the expense of the banks' lending to private individuals and companies. That certainly wouldn't please the banks—who would lose a lot of profitable business. And the drastic cut back in bank lending to the rest of us would have very severe implications which we shall look at in a moment.

However, there remains a different sort of reason why governments have been rightly suspicious of the Monetarist medicine. The argument that it is too much money which *causes* inflation remains unproved. All that the Monetarists have so far done is to show that in the past they have moved in the same direction. And doubt remains, too, about precisely *how* controlling the money supply would stop prices rising.

In this situation, governments face a double danger in pinning their hopes on the Monetarist prescription.

EITHER   they might find that it didn't work, and that the Monetarist analysis of the cause and cure for inflation was, after all, wrong.

OR   it did work in checking price increases—but at what was regarded as an intolerably high cost.

Doubt about whether limiting the money supply would be effective in curbing spending stems from the flexibility which exists in a sophisticated financial system like ours. A limited quantity of money might simply be made to work harder, and circulate more rapidly. In the same way that in our earlier example, Christmas spending could still take place even if the Bank of England didn't increase the note issue, so also higher spending in the economy might be sustained with a relatively fixed money supply—by either using existing forms of credit more exhaustively or introducing new ones.

If it did work, if limiting the growth of the money supply was *not* offset in these ways, then *how* would it work? If over-spending *was* the cause of inflation and price increases could be halted by more monetary discipline, it would work through making it more difficult for individuals and firms to borrow from the banks. We could spend less as a result and so many firms, particularly the smaller ones which are heavily reliant on the banks for their working capital, would be bound to make their employees redundant. But how much unemployment would be needed to bring inflation under control? Five per cent out of work? Or ten per cent? That is a vital question to which there is no certain answer—as we shall see in the next chapter.

What, then, causes inflation? There are two broad views, and many variants of them. There are those who think that rising prices are caused by *cost-push*—and argue amongst themselves about which of the pushing costs is the most important—and there are the Monetarists who argue that cost increases are only a symptom of the excessive *money* which they claim is at the root of inflation.

We love to blame governments for their incompetence in dealing with our economic problems, but it is difficult not to sympathise with them as they try to grapple with inflation without knowing precisely what causes it. It's not that they are short of expert advice. Advice is plentiful but conflicting.

Would limiting the money supply work?

Gross Profits of the 'Big Four' Banks, 1973

£190 million
National Westminster

£185 million
Barclays

£131 million
Lloyds

£110 million
Midland

And if non-economists are disappointed that our discussion of inflation so far hasn't pointed to any simple explanation of why prices rise and what to do about them, they should remember that it is in just this context of controversy and uncertainty that governments have to make their decisions. It is as important to be aware of the limitations of economics—of what economists *don't* know—as it is to understand what they *do* know.

MONETARIST ECONOMICS

The monetarists' case can be summarised as follows:

■ Inflation is caused by the government putting too much money into circulation. . . . *therefore*

■ the government should restrict the supply of money in the economy. . . . *with the result that*

■ this would reduce inflation without too much harm being done in the process.

Each of the three stages of the argument can be challenged. Can you say what the objections are?

Answer:

■ Increased availability of money may not be the cause of inflation at all—the cause may lie elsewhere.

■ This is more easily said than done. The government would have to raise money for its own needs in some other way—probably by higher taxation—if it cut back on its own borrowing.

Besides, alternative sources of money and credit could spring up outside the main banks, and quite possibly outside government control.

■ Great harm might be caused as a result of restricting the availability of money if unemployment rose to an unacceptable level, or if government spending was slashed leaving social services depleted.

IS 3 MILLION UNEMPLOYED THE ANSWER?

*BEWARE OF THOSE WHO COME UP WITH KILL-OR-CURE SOLUTIONS. THEY **CAN** KILL AND NEED NOT CURE.*

Do *you* believe that a dose of unemployment would help to curb inflation?

IF YOUR ANSWER IS *YES*

■ is it because you think more unemployment would bring the unions to heel and reduce wage claims?

■ or is it because you think unemployment would cut total spending and stop 'too much money chasing too few goods'?

■ how big a dose of unemployment would be needed?

■ are you sure you're not arguing for more unemployment in the safe knowledge that it won't affect *you* personally?

IF YOUR ANSWER IS *NO*:

■ is it because the costs of large-scale unemployment are too great?

■ if so, are you thinking primarily of *economic* or *social* costs?

■ or is it because you don't believe the unemployment medicine would work?

■ or is it that you think unemployment is unfair on those whose jobs are at risk—particularly if you think you fall into that description yourself?

In this chapter the arguments for and against 'a dose of unemployment' are considered.

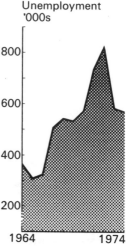

Unemployment '000s

There are many people who believe that the economy is now set on a disaster course towards runaway inflation and who will dismiss the discussion of the last two chapters about what causes inflation as academic fiddling while Rome burns. Such is the hold of the inflationary cancer, they say, that only the most drastic surgery will provide a cure. They plead for a strong government with the courage to bring the economy to its senses by purging it with a painful dose of unemployment. Only then can we begin to reconstruct it on more orderly lines.

This gut reaction on the part of certain sections of the community is supported by the arguments of some economists. For them, too, we have to *choose* between stable prices and unemployment.

Which is worse, inflation or unemployment?

We worry about inflation because

■ of the difficulty in keeping up with it,

■ it eats away at our savings,

■ it reduces our international competitiveness,

■ it makes the future so uncertain.

And lurking in the wings is the spectre of prices soaring to banana republic proportions, and of the financial system totally collapsing under the strain of runaway inflation. Just how much inflation worries *you* must partly depend on *your* place in the economic jigsaw—your job, how much you earn, how old you are, how much you save and how strong your bargaining position is.

But unemployment is also fearful.

■ It strikes directly at the living standards of those thrown out of work.

■ It undermines the human dignity of those who are denied the opportunity of working to support themselves and their families.

■ It is an obvious economic waste: costly State benefits and lost production.
■ It aggravates social tensions.

How much *you* worry about rising unemployment depends partly on your moral response, and partly on the chances of *you* becoming one of the workless. Do you live in the North, do you work in a growing or declining industry, how old are you, what colour are you? All of these considerations are relevant to whether you would be lucky enough to keep your job.

WHO ARE THE UNEMPLOYED?
■ In March 1975 800,000 people were registered as unemployed in the U.K. (3½% of workers). One in five of these were women.
■ The chances of a man being unemployed (1 in 22) were three times greater than for women (1 in 62).
■ The greatest number of unemployed were to be found in services and engineering.
■ The chances of being unemployed were, however, greatest in construction (1 in 8). Unemployment was also high (1 in 20) in metal goods; food, drink and tobacco; textiles and mining.
■ The chances of finding a job again were high in engineering, mining and chemicals,

but low in agriculture and construction.
■ Job chances were generally far better for manual than for white-collar workers.
■ Two out of every three unemployed had been without jobs for more than two months; one in four of them had been unemployed for more than a year.
■ Prospects of finding a job deteriorate the longer a person remains on the register. Job prospects are also significantly worse for older workers.
■ There was a rather higher rate of unemployment for black workers than the average.
■ Unemployment among the disabled was particularly high (1 in 10).

Inflation versus unemployment

But if inflation and unemployment are *both* evils, which is the worse? To try to find the answer, suppose that it can be shown, beyond all doubt, that inflation is controllable only through higher unemployment. Then is that a price worth paying? Imagine that you are presented with a range of firm alternatives. Just how much unemployment would you find acceptable to get just what reduction in the rate of inflation?

Rate of inflation	Number unemployed
25%	½ million
20%	1 million
15%	1¼ million
10%	2 million
5%	3 million
0	4 million

Which combination would YOU choose?

Your choice depends partly on your personal and political values, and partly on how you judge the economic ill-effects of the twin evils of inflation and unemployment. It probably also reflects a mixture of self-interest and a notion of what you think is needed in the national interest.

It is a very painful choice, but just the sort that governments have to make when faced with the possibility that their policy objectives are incompatible. But their difficulties, as we have already seen, are compounded by the ignorance of economists. Not only are economists unable to present governments with precise 'trade-offs' between inflation and unemployment. They are far from unanimous that there *is* any trade-off between the two. The relationship between prices and employment is an area of profound disagreement between almost all economists.

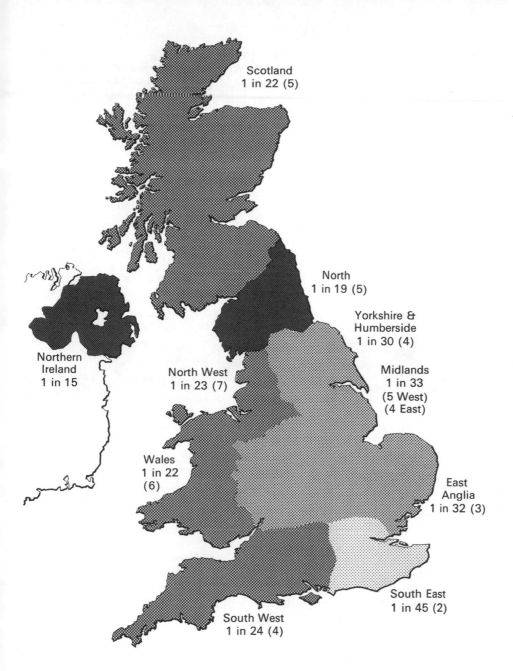

Scotland
1 in 22 (5)

North
1 in 19 (5)

Yorkshire &
Humberside
1 in 30 (4)

Northern
Ireland
1 in 15

North West
1 in 23 (7)

Midlands
1 in 33
(5 West)
(4 East)

Wales
1 in 22
(6)

East
Anglia
1 in 32 (3)

South East
1 in 45 (2)

South West
1 in 24 (4)

WHERE ARE THE UNEMPLOYED?

The greatest number of unemployed is in the South East (165,000 in March 1975). But there were more workers—and also more vacancies—in the South East than anywhere else. The chances of being without a job were therefore lower in the South East than other areas. The map shows both the chances of being unemployed, and in brackets the number of workers chasing each vacancy, in each region.

The map conceals even greater variations. Unemployment can be as low as 1 in 125 (as in Hertford), or as high as 1 in 16 (Dumbarton), 1 in 14 (Wrexham), 1 in 13 (Sunderland) or even 1 in 6 (Newry, Northern Ireland).

In areas of high unemployment, the chances of being unemployed were especially high for the disabled and for young people.

The Times recently summarised the views of several leading economists which had been put together in a book.*
To the question:
'What is the chief sign of our economic difficulties?'
nine economists said inflation;
two said balance of payments;
two said a combination of both;
and only two said recession.

But to the question:
'What is the chief cause of our problems?'
four said the government's obsession with full employment;
three said bad economic policy;
three said oil prices or wages;
and two said our failure to sell to oil countries.

* *The Times*, January 31, 1975, page 14.
Crisis '75 (Institute of Economic Affairs)

The main reason why economists disagree is that they are much better at thinking up theories than going out and seeing whether they fit the facts of the real world. If Professor X asserts that a million and half unemployed would halve the rate of inflation and Professor Y disputes this, then in principle their argument can be settled by seeing what actually happens when unemployment rises to that level. However, in practice, governments are hardly likely to throw people out of work just to satisfy the intellectual curiosity of economists, and even if unemployment did rise to Professor X's figure and the rate of inflation was halved, it would still be open to Professor Y to argue that it wasn't unemployment which had done the trick, but some other factor.

The economy is not a laboratory in which economists can perform their experiments in controlled conditions. Instead, they have to rely on scraps of historical and contemporary evidence which don't generally lend themselves to one simple interpretation. Given these difficulties under which they labour, economists should not be too much blamed for their failure to provide copper-bottomed answers to the questions which concern us. Indeed, if anything, they should rather be blamed for too often giving the impression of *knowing* when in fact they are only *theorising*. It is important to keep these limitations of economic expertise in mind in looking at the case for and against unemployment as a means of checking rising prices.

The case for unemployment as a cure for inflation

Higher unemployment to curb price increases has been proposed by economists holding very different views about the causes of inflation.

■ Amongst those who see wage-push as the main cause are some who argue that therefore the greater the number out of work, the less will be the power or willingness of trade unions to press inflationary wage claims. On this view, it is the way in which postwar governments have felt obliged to keep the level of spending in the economy high enough to sustain full employment which has enabled unions to demand higher wages without the fear that some of their members will be made jobless as a result.

The main evidence to support this case is that in the past there has been a very close statistical relationship between the level of unemployment and the rate of increase in money wages (a connexion which held good remarkably constantly over a long period of time until, as we shall see, it underwent a sea-change after the mid-sixties). This so-called 'Phillips curve relationship' suggested that modest increases in unemployment would be sufficient to slow down the rate of wage increases—and, therefore, if wages were the root of the trouble, the rate of inflation.

NOW YOU SEE IT...

The 'Phillips curve' represents the link between the level of unemployment and the size of wage increases. The lower the level of unemployment, the faster wages rise, whilst when there are more unemployed wages increase much more slowly.

The relationship, which suggests that excess demand for labour pushes up wages, is based upon figures for the 'fifties and early 'sixties. During that period it seemed clear that wages rose more when there were fewer unemployed; high levels of unemployment seemed linked with smaller wage rises:

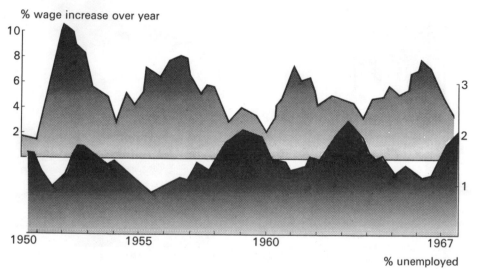

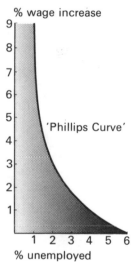

■ Support for higher unemployment also comes, as we saw in Chapter 2, from economists who think that it is an excessive money supply rather than trade unions which is the real cause of inflation. For them, regulating the economy via the money supply would reduce the pressure of demand by cutting government overspending and squeezing less efficient firms out of business. The Monetarist policy would mean that the number out of work might increase substantially in the short run, and then settle down after a while at a level appropriate for an economy running with stable prices.

So, for the wage-pushers, higher unemployment is the way to hit at union bargaining power and militancy, And for the money-men, it is the incidental by-product of monetary discipline aimed at limiting spending in the economy.

Would a large pool of unemployed make the unions moderate their demands as they came to recognise that excessive wage claims threatened jobs? Experience in the late sixties and early seventies casts doubt on whether this

The case against unemployment as a cure for inflation

would happen. This was the period when the Phillips curve relationship broke down. Higher unemployment became accompanied by greater rather than smaller increases in wage-rates. It is possible that once governments are seen to be following a policy of deliberately allowing unemployment to rise, the effect is to make trade unions more militant still. The end result could be the worst of both worlds: higher unemployment *and* even more rapid inflation.

IF THEY THREATEN US WITH THE DOLE, THEN THE CHIPS WILL REALLY BE DOWN.

...NOW YOU DON'T!
Since 1967 the link between pay and unemployment seems to have gone into reverse. Fewer unemployed now seems to go with lower wage rises, and we have recently experienced record post-war unemployment at the same time as record increases in wages.

Like the wage-pushers, the Monetarists base their case on statistical evidence—they point out that price rises have closely followed expansion in the money supply. But what they cannot demonstrate is what would have happened if the money supply had been held back. If ever it were, then the relation between prices and the money supply might be destroyed. Firms and unions might respond to the shortage of money in a totally new and unexpected way—for example, unions becoming more aggressive, firms finding new sources of credit. Therefore, what past experience suggests would be the appropriate level of unemployment might be well below the amount needed in the quite different conditions brought about by a policy of monetary discipline.

Again, unemployment may be ineffective in curbing inflation because one of its side-effects would be to leave firms with excess capacity. That is, they would find that the factories and machines in which they had invested when expecting a high level of demand for their products would not, after all, be fully used. They would therefore have to recoup their expesive overheads from a smaller volume of sales—and this, in itself, would give a new cost-inflationary push to prices. Moreover, the damage caused in the process to business confidence might prove very difficult to repair subsequently.

A VIRTUOUS CIRCLE

There has been a close relationship between the rate at which our national output has increased, and the rate at which output per worker (or productivity) has improved. The moral seems to be that expansion brings with it greater efficiency; unemployment thus appears even more costly.

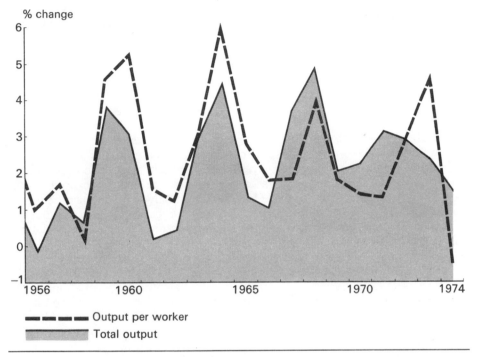

% change

- - - - Output per worker

▨ Total output

Unemployment is basically wasteful. It means forfeiting potential output while at the same time maintaining the incomes of those out of work at a socially tolerable level. It is also likely to have a highly concentrated impact on the already less prosperous parts of the economy. Experience shows that whenever unemployment increases nationally, the poorer areas of the country are relatively worse hit. Trying to control inflation through higher unemployment would intensify an already serious regional problem. Those living in 'development areas' would be the chief victims of policies aimed at dampening down wage increases and spending in the more booming regions.

More positively, it can be argued that only if governments maintain full employment (and, indeed, get the economy on to an expansionary path) can they hope to command general acceptance for measures aimed at regulating prices and incomes or bringing about structural changes in the economy. And the fact that they have not been successful in the past does not mean that further attempts to make them work should now be abandoned in favour of punitive unemployment for which the case remains unproved.

How do governments come to a policy decision on a matter as vitally important for us all as the one which we have just been discussing ? They have to approach

it at a number of levels.

■ Faced with conflicting advice, which of the economic experts should they believe? Economists do not *know* the precise causes of inflation or the effects of the policies which they recommend. They can only estimate the probabilities that alternative explanations and cures are the right ones and even then they will often disagree.

■ All governments are concerned with political expediency. They all want to stay in power. Inflation and unemployment are *both* unpopular. If a government is persuaded that they are alternatives, then it might ask—which is likely to lose more votes? Everyone is more or less affected by rising prices while unemployment hits directly at relatively few. But unemployment, on the other hand, carries with it the opprobrium of a 'return to the thirties', could lead to industrial confrontation, and worsen a variety of social problems such as race relations and disparities between the regions.

■ Finally, issues like this must be resolved in the light of the political principles to which the different parties subscribe. Even if a government is convinced by its advisers that higher unemployment would help to abate inflation, it still has to decide what relative values it should attach to the misery of those thrown out of work compared with the benefits for those lucky enough to hold on to their jobs and enjoy more stable prices.

This is the sort of question put to *you* at the beginning of the chapter. Governments have to answer it—and act accordingly.

That in the case of inflation in particular, they have not been very successful is perhaps not surprising in view of the inadequacies of economic knowledge and techniques of control which we have been stressing. More lamentable is the fact that governments have not therefore done more in compensating for the *effects* of inflation. That is the theme of the next two chapters.

THE COSTS OF UNEMPLOYMENT

Every time someone becomes unemployed, all kinds of costs are involved:

■ To the *unemployed themselves*, in the form of reduced income, loss of savings, etc.

■ To *national output*, in the form of lost production and possibly exports.

■ Loss to *other companies and workers*, in the form of repercussion effects on nearby and related jobs, contracts, etc.

■ Loss to the *government* of tax revenue which it would have collected from the worker, as well as the costs of redundancy payments (a cost to the firm as well), unemployment benefit and supplementary assistance.

It has been estimated:

■ that it would cost a total of £900 million in unemployment and social security benefits if there were a million unemployed

■ and that if redundancy pay and the loss of tax revenue were also counted, then a doubling of unemployment from around 600,000 to $1\frac{1}{4}$ million would mean that the government's borrowing requirement would rise by a further £800-£850 million.

WINNERS AND LOSERS

IN THE STRUGGLE TO KEEP UP WITH INFLATION SOME ARE MUCH MORE SUCCESSFUL THAN OTHERS. IT'S OFTEN HIGHLY UNFAIR.

THE POUND IN YOUR POCKET

Compared with what it would buy in 1962, £1 in 1975 was worth only 43½ pence. But apart from this reduced purchasing power, consider:

■ If your income rises by 20% and prices also rise by 20%, does this mean that you've kept up with inflation?
Does your answer take into account:
The amount of extra tax you have to pay?
The pattern of your family's spending?

The level of State benefits, and your own entitlement to them?
■ Who has been best placed to keep up with inflation: has the car worker or the old age pensioner had the bigger percentage increase over the past few years?
These are some of the questions concerning the effects of inflation upon different groups of people which are looked at in this chapter.

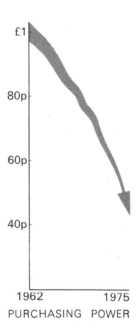

PURCHASING POWER

While the argument rages about precisely why prices rise, and governments try one policy after another to stop them doing so, the rest of us meanwhile have to learn to live with the *effects* of inflation. We all complain, but with very different cause for complaint. Inflation affects different sections of the community in ways which, when they are brought out into the open, most of us would think undesirable and unfair, and governments have been only partially successful in preventing this from happening.

Economists used to say that people judged how well off they were by looking at their *money* incomes. So long as *they* continued to grow, they felt better off even though, if prices were rising faster, they were nothing of the sort. However, these days there can't be many who still fall for this 'money illusion'. Rapid inflation has made us all a bit wiser and aware that we should distinguish between money and *real* income. Real income measures what can be bought with money income—and it's real income that counts. Nobody any longer thinks that he is better off with a wage rise of 10% if prices meanwhile have gone up 20%. Despite his rise, his wages won't go so far; his real income will have fallen. Something has to go: smoking or a summer holiday or the Sunday joint.

On first sight, the figures suggest that we have beaten inflation hands down. For example, between 1963 and 1974, average earnings rose by 161% while prices meanwhile increased less than 100%. However, the picture looks far less rosy when it is remembered that:

■ After deductions, real take-home pay during this period only grew by some 1% per annum.

■ Over these years, the economy was producing about 2-3% more output each year—so that we might have expected to be substantially better off.

■ These are, anyway, only average figures. Some groups fared far less well than others.

How well *you* have managed to keep up with rising prices partly depends on the way in which your income is determined.

It might be that your income is fixed *administratively*—if, for example you are young or old and rely on a student grant or State retirement pension. You might be able to bring some pressure to bear, but in the end it is the government of the day which decides when and by how much your income will rise.

Or are your wages the result of *collective bargaining* between your union and your employer? If so, is it a strong union, and are you working in an industry which is crucial to the rest of the economy? Or are you weakly organised— perhaps in a workforce mostly made up of women or of those who think that industrial action is unethical? Do you work in the private sector or for the government or a nationalised industry? Or aren't you a member of a union at all, and just bargain with your employer on your own account? And how important to you is the difference between wage-rates and earnings: what are the prospects of short-time or overtime working, bonuses and part-time ways of adding to your basic income?

And finally, it might be *you* who determines your own income—if, for example, you sell your services directly to the public like vets or hairdressers or accountants do. Or perhaps you are a company director and on a management board which decides what its members should be paid.

In an inflationary free-for-all, everything depends on the luck of the draw: the industry in which you happen to work, your bargaining power and the way your pay is determined. In the process, only justice will be done incidentally. The strong will be able to defend themselves against rising prices and the weak will lag behind.

Consider, for example, which of the following is likely to cope best with inflation: car workers, top managers, electricity supply workers, engine drivers, coal miners, civil servants, farmworkers, pensioners, nurses and bus drivers. It might be expected that the first five would do relatively well—either because of their strategic bargaining strength or because they fixed their own incomes—and the others would be the ones who slipped behind. The facts of the matter are surprisingly different.

THE PAY LEAGUE TABLE
Pay rise, 1970-1974

Division One		Division Two	
(Above average wage increase, above average price increase)	%	(Below average wage increase, above average price increase)	%
Old age pensioners	100	Civil servants	59
Farmworkers	81	Car workers	50
Coal miners	80	Engine drivers	50
Electricity supply workers	79	INFLATION	46
ALL WORKERS AVERAGE	61		

Division Three	
(Below average wage increase, below average price increase)	%
Top managers	45
Bus drivers (London Transport)	44
Nurses	42

The difference between how you might have expected these groups to do and what has actually happened is some indication of the extent to which governments have tried to minimise the unfair effects on income distribution which inflation is likely to cause. The results may be far from perfect. The fact that pensioners and farmworkers have enjoyed large percentage increases over these years tells us nothing about whether their *levels* of income can be regarded as satisfactory. Although most of us might agree that it was right that coal miners should improve their relative position, would we also accept that nurses and bus drivers should have become worse off?

INCOMES POLICIES AND LOW PAY

Incomes policies

PRICES AND INCOMES POLICY
(Labour) 1965:
Low paid workers were to qualify for exceptional treatment *'where there is general recognition that existing wage and salary levels are too low to maintain a reasonable standard of living'.*

COUNTER-INFLATION PROGRAMME
(Conservative) 1973:
Stage Two (third general principle):
'to facilitate an improvement in the relative position of the low paid.'

Stage Three (underlying principle):
'In the interests of fairness, the Government propose to make special provision to help the low paid. . . .'

SOCIAL CONTRACT (Labour/TUC) 1974:
'priority should also be given to attaining reasonable minimum standards, including the TUC's low pay target of a £25 minimum basic rate with higher minimum earnings, for a normal week for those aged 18 and over.'

Barbara Castle

Ted Heath

Len Murray

Incomes policies although aimed chiefly at limiting pay increases, have also been used by governments to introduce elements of social justice into the system of income determination. However, there is practically no evidence that incomes policies have substantially helped the system of tax allowances. If they didn't, then inflation and rising incomes would automatically push larger and larger numbers into the tax-paying category for the first time. To counter this, what governments have done is regularly to raise the 'tax threshold' at which tax first becomes payable.

Tax allowances

TAX THRESHOLD
The level of income at which you first begin to pay income tax is known as the 'tax threshold', and is determined by the values of the various tax allowances. For a family with two children under 11 the tax threshold in 1964 was £736 annually. Governments have raised this up to a level of £1,383 in 1975: that is, they have almost doubled it.

But this doubling is only in money terms.

When inflation over this period is taken into account the real value of the tax threshold in 1975 is only £602. In real terms it has not increased at all, but has fallen by 18% from its 1964 level.

On top of this, the family now starts to pay tax at the full rate of 35 pence for every £ above the threshold, whereas up to 1970 there were special reduced rates of tax for the first slices of taxable income.

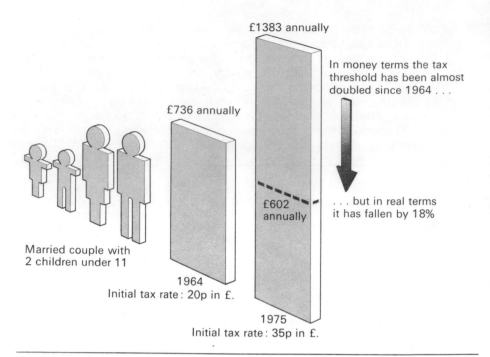

£1383 annually

In money terms the tax threshold has been almost doubled since 1964 . . .

£736 annually

. . . but in real terms it has fallen by 18%

£602 annually

Married couple with 2 children under 11

1964
Initial tax rate: 20p in £.

1975
Initial tax rate: 35p in £.

State benefits

Thirdly governments can try to protect people's living standards against the impact of inflation is by revising the levels of State benefits which they pay to different groups.

However, the system of benefits and tax allowances can, in times of inflation, combine to force low-paid members of the community into what has become known as the 'poverty trap'. This happens when a pay increase gained by the breadwinner of the family is cancelled out by a loss of entitlement to benefits as the income cut-off point is reached.

BENEFITS AND ALLOWANCES
There are two kinds of benefits and allowances available:

■ those to which everyone is entitled, regardless of income level, such as family allowances and retirement pensions; these are known as *universal* benefits;
■ those which involve an income qualification, such as free school meals or family income supplement; these are called *selective* or *means-tested* benefits.

Family allowances were increased in 1968, to 90p per week for the second child and £1 for subsequent children. By 1975 inflation had reduced their *real* value to about 50p per week.

There are over 40 means-tested benefits altogether, the main ones being family income supplement, free school meals, rent and rate rebates and allowances, and free prescription charges, dental and optical treatment. Family income supplement is payable to families where the breadwinner is in full-time work and family income falls below certain levels set by the government. The other benefits also depend on your level of income and the number of children you have.

THE POVERTY TRAP
If a married man with two children is earning £28 a week and then gets a pay rise of £4 he can stand to lose the following benefits:

School meals worth 60p weekly for each child	£1.20
Family Income Supplement worth	£1.00
Free health treatment worth	20
Rent rebate	70
Total	£3.10

On top of this he would pay tax now and extra national insurance contributions, so losing a further £1.60. The combined effect of all this is to turn what was originally a £4 gain into a 70 pence loss.

Governments have also controlled or subsidised some of the prices which hit particularly hard at those living on low budgets. The unfairness of inflation is not just to do with pay. It also stems from the different ways in which we spend our incomes. Although the pattern of spending varies enormously from one family to another, there are certain items which appear in every family budget. We all face bills for food, housing, lighting and fuel. Low income groups spend a far greater proportion of their incomes on these necessities than those higher up the scale and are therefore much worse hit when, as in recent years, it is the prices of these basics which have been amongst the fastest risers.

Prices of necessities

FAMILY EXPENDITURE

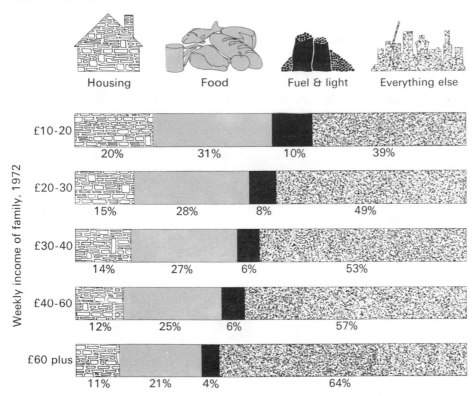

	Housing	Food	Fuel & light	Everything else
£10-20	20%	31%	10%	39%
£20-30	15%	28%	8%	49%
£30-40	14%	27%	6%	53%
£40-60	12%	25%	6%	57%
£60 plus	11%	21%	4%	64%

Weekly income of family, 1972

HOW DIFFERENT PRICES HAVE RISEN:
Usually the basic items go up fastest in price. In 1971 inflation would have been only 6½%, without the increases in the three basics.

1974 was quite different. The government was not able—and did not choose—to hold back fuel prices. But its policies of rent controls and food subsidies held down the price increases of food and housing.

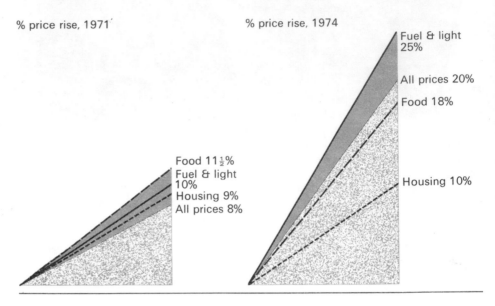

% price rise, 1971

Food 11½%
Fuel & light 10%
Housing 9%
All prices 8%

% price rise, 1974

Fuel & light 25%
All prices 20%
Food 18%
Housing 10%

To sum up, then, government policies—with regard to tax thresholds, benefits and allowances, and prices—mean that it is not simply the increase in your *gross* pay which determine whether you are a winner or loser in the battle with rising prices. And two further factors may have an important bearing on how you fare.

Income tax

Income tax is generally levied progressively, i.e. the higher the income, the higher the *rate* (and not just the *amount*) of tax deducted. However, for the £4,500 of income immediately above the tax threshold, the same standard rate applies and a pay increase within this wide range will not therefore subject whoever gets it to the same jumps in the rate of tax payable which affect others.

Tax rate

TAX HOLLOW

Income level

Some people are helped to become winners rather than losers by virtue of receiving fringe benefits from their employer which really represent tax-free income in a lot of cases.

The inflationary game is one in which there are few winners but many losers. If they are unable to halt inflation, then governments need to pay a lot of attention to devising ways of avoiding its unwanted and undesirable effects on the distribution of income; and they have become increasingly conscious of this need. They have provided benefits and subsidies as a cushion against rising prices, National Insurance contributions are now wholly earnings-related, and the Family Income Supplement now remains payable for a year after a worker's wage increases takes him beyond the cut-off point. However, there is still scope for further measures like tying tax thresholds and family allowances automatically to increases in the cost of living and in reintroducing more gradually increasing rates of taxation at the lower end of the scale.

Trade unions, too, have a part to play. Some of them already have a good record of building into their wage negotiations protection for those worst hit by inflation—even though it has meant smaller increases for their better paid members. What remains missing though, is any mechanism by which (perhaps through the TUC) restraint by the more powerful unions can be translated into better provision for those less favourably placed.

There are a lucky few who have done well out of inflation, but they are not always those whom most people would think should be the gainers. And in the next chapter, we look at another morally questionable result of inflation—that those who borrow have prospered at the expense of those who save.

FRINGE BENEFITS

For someone earning £25,000 per annum and paying the top rate of income tax, fringe benefits are more valuable than extra salary. If he enjoyed all the following most typical fringe benefits, they would be the equivalent of a £20,000 salary increase.

Fringe benefit	Value up to:
housing (low interest loans, etc.)	£800
car (vehicle itself and running costs)	£2,200
school fees for children	£380
holiday provided	£400
telephone	£70
general expenses	£200
dress and entertainment	£100
top-hat pensions, golden handshakes	£200
Total	£4,350

The value of the fringe benefits rises with inflation, whereas the value of basic salary falls.

FLAT-RATE FAIRNESS?

Since inflation affects the distribution of income unfairly, what can be done about it? Here are two proposals:

■ give everyone the same *percentage* increase in pay. This would maintain differentials and incentives for the better off.

■ give everyone the same flat-rate *money* increase in pay. This would ensure that the broadest backs would bear the biggest sacrifices.

Here are the effects of the two proposals upon the pay of:
a worker on half average earnings;
a worker on average earnings;
a worker on twice average earnings.

	20% increase	£10 flat-rate increase money	As %
½ average earnings (£25)	£5	£10	40%
average earnings (£50)	£10	£10	20%
twice average earnings (£100)	£20	£10	10%

THE SAVINGS SCANDAL

> GOVERNMENTS HAVE PREACHED HOW IMPORTANT IT IS FOR THE ECONOMY THAT WE SHOULD SAVE. AND THEY HAVE ALLOWED SAVINGS TO BE DESTROYED BY INFLATION.

WHEN DID YOU LAST SEE YOUR SAVINGS?

£100 put away at the beginning of 1974 would be worth little more than £80 by the end of the year as a result of inflation.

■ Were you a saver in 1974?

If you were, you were almost certainly playing a losing game. There was no usual form of saving which could have provided a return for you great enough to match inflation.

■ But perhaps you were a borrower in 1974?

In that case it is certain that the rate of interest you paid your bank or building society was less than inflation, so that you were on the winning side.

Whether you personally gained or lost in the saving/borrowing game, do you find it acceptable that this state of affairs should exist? Is it fair that governments should do little or nothing to help the suffering saver, whilst continuing to allow borrowers the benefit of tax relief in some cases? Apart from fairness, does it make any economic sense to leave the savers to go to the wall? This chapter examines the plight of the saver and what can be done to help him.

Those who have saved have been penalised for their thriftiness by inflation, and governments have done little to protect them. Those, on the other hand, who have borrowed up to the hilt have often done very well indeed. That is the savings scandal.

Year by year, inflation has first nibbled, then gnawed and finally begun to swallow great slices of the value of savings. By 1975, £100 saved in a tin box since 1965 bought only half as much it did ten years earlier because meanwhile prices had doubled.

People no longer look for a good rate of return on their savings. The problem has become one of trying to maintain their real purchasing power. Before the seventies, savings with an institution like a building society rather than in a tin box helped in this respect because, while the value of savings was being eroded by inflation at 3-4% a year, this was generally more than offset by the amount of interest earned. But in recent years this has no longer been the case. Although money rates of interest have at times reached record levels, they have been far below the current rate of inflation. Even an after-tax return as high as 10% is obviously nothing like enough to protect savings from the destructive effects of price increases in excess of 25%. The real rate of interest has become *negative*.

> THERE'S NOTHING LEFT TO SAVE BY THE TIME I'VE MADE ENDS MEET.

HOW A *REAL* RATE OF INTEREST CAN BE NEGATIVE

The interest rate on a building society deposit account during 1974 was 7¼%, so that £100 deposited during the year would nominally have risen to £107.25. However prices rose by 20% in 1974, so that the real value of the £107.25 was reduced to £89.50. The real interest rate was thus a negative one: minus 10½%.

It is surprising that there is not more of a public outcry about the savings scandal. Perhaps that is because it is felt to be a problem only for the better-off—those who can *afford* to save. But although we may not make regular deposits at a bank or with a building society, *most* of us do in fact save. Contributing to a pension scheme, holding a life assurance policy, putting something aside for a summer holiday, buying Premium Bonds or simply being a member of a Christmas Club—are all ways of saving. We do it on quite a big scale. Total personal saving in the U.K. has recently been running at over £5,000 million a year. That means that on average we have been putting aside one pound out of every ten that we earn.

The savings scandal does affect a very large number of us whether we realise it or not. For example, six million people in this country are members of a private pension scheme. Many such schemes are now in a state of acute crisis.

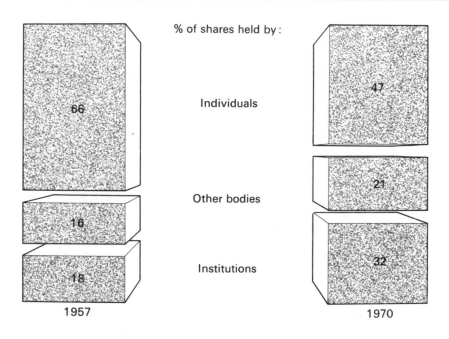

% of shares held by:

Individuals

Other bodies

Institutions

1957   1970

SHOULD YOU BE IN AN INSTITUTION?
Since the war more and more people have saved with life insurance companies and pension funds, rather than by saving personally and directly.
Since 1950:
■ life insurance funds have increased seven times
■ pension funds have increased twelve times
■ unit trusts have increased even more rapidly.
This means more people have become shareholders—even though only indirectly—since the pension fund, etc., invests a large part of their money in stocks and shares.

This has altered the way in which stocks and shares are distributed.
In 1957:
■ 2 out of every 3 shares were owned by individuals;
■ less than 1 in 5 shares was held by the institutions.
In 1970:
■ less than half of all shares were individually held;
■ more than 1 in 3 shares was held by the institutions.
Nevertheless of those shares held by individuals 93% are held by only 5% of the population.

The Pensions Crisis

The object of a pensions scheme is to accumulate a fund large enough to finance retirement pensions related to the members' earnings. The fund consists of two parts: contributions from members plus the interest which is earned by investing them. Normally, the build-up of the fund would follow this sort of pattern over a member's working life:

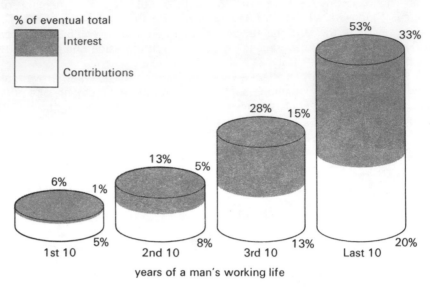

years of a man's working life

Not much happens during the first ten years. The member's earnings are low—and so therefore are his contributions and the interest earned on them. Both increase during the second and third decades, and interest earned on past contributions forms an increasing proportion of the total. What is interesting, however, is that after thirty years, three-quarters of the member's working life, the fund has accumulated less than half the total amount required. The rest comes in the final ten years—partly from higher contributions but mostly from interest.

If inflation suddenly accelerates as it has done, the pensions scheme's calculations are completely undermined. Members' incomes have increased with inflation and they expect correspondingly higher pensions. But there is no way in which the necessary funds can be accumulated. The increase in contributions which would be needed is prohibitively large, and the vital interest component, as we have seen, has been reduced in recent years to negative proportions.

What this means is that, if inflation continues as it has, millions of people will find that their retirement pensions, for which they have saved over the years, will be worth far less than they expected.

Who's suffered most?

The two main victims of inflation are those whom fairness might have suggested should be best protected—small savers and those who have lent to the government.

What can the small saver do with his money? There's the Post Office, National Savings and building societies, for example—all of which promise him that his savings will be *safe* with them. That is quite true in the sense that governments and building societies seldom go bust, but what has happened to the real value of £100 deposited with each of them in 1965? Ten years later, the Post Office deposits with interest will have grown to £128, National Savings to £145, and the deposit with a building society to £164; but with prices doubling meanwhile, their purchasing power has fallen between 18-36%.

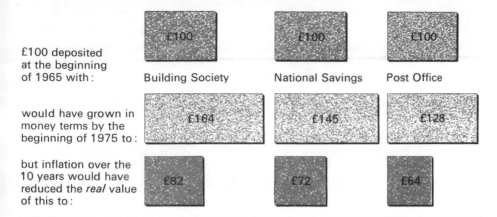

£100 deposited at the beginning of 1965 with:

Building Society   **National Savings**   **Post Office**

would have grown in money terms by the beginning of 1975 to:

but inflation over the 10 years would have reduced the *real* value of this to:

As it can be seen, it is the combination of being a small saver who lends to the government which is the worst of all. But governments also borrow large sums through the stock market, and those who have held government bonds have similarly found that their savings have been ravaged by inflation.

The total of outstanding government borrowing is called the National Debt. Most of it was incurred in times of war. Since 1945, however, governments have also become net borrowers in peace time, spending far more than they have been able or willing to raise through taxation. And governments in the past have offered no protection against inflation to those from whom they have borrowed. £100 lent to the government is repaid as £100 whenever the loan matures— regardless of how much its real worth may have fallen in the meantime.

THE SMALL SAVER

If the typical small saver is taken as someone with wealth between £1,000 and £3,000, then Inland Revenue figures provide the following picture of how he saves: the basic forms of saving account together for nearly two-thirds of his savings, whilst only £2 in every £100 is held by small savers in stocks and shares.

The stock market is not a practicable place for the small saver, since the various costs involved in share trading (stamp duty, brokerage, taxes, etc.) can amount to half the face value of a share or bond. This is one reason for the growth of the institutions.

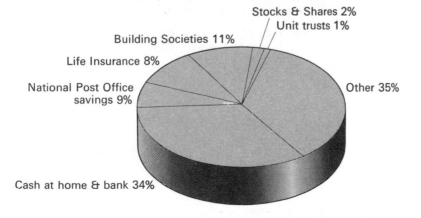

Stocks & Shares 2%
Unit trusts 1%
Building Societies 11%
Life Insurance 8%
National Post Office savings 9%
Other 35%
Cash at home & bank 34%

What is more, should the saver want to cash in *before* the loan matures—by selling his bonds in the stock market—the price he will get is probably far less than their nominal £100 value. That is because, in order to borrow more, governments have had to offer higher and higher interest rates. Therefore, if the present rate they are offering is 10%, then holders of bonds issued some years earlier at 5% will obviously only be able to find buyers for them at very much lower prices than they paid for them.

The better off have wider opportunities to make their savings pay—like buying equities or company shares. These can be expected to offer some safeguard against inflation because, when prices rise, so generally do profits and the value of the land, factories and machines employed by firms.

However, even holding shares is a risky business because of the way in which their prices fluctuate. Someone who bought shares in 1962 and sold them ten years later would have beaten inflation by a good 20%; but if they had held on to 1974, when share prices had fallen drastically, they would have suffered a real loss of 40%. Hedging against inflation is difficult for everybody, except perhaps the lucky few who combine the wealth and the specialist knowledge needed to accumulate Old Masters, antiques or stamp collections.

THE BIG SAVER

At the other extreme from the small saver is the person with wealth between £100,000 and £200,000. Inland Revenue figures show the make-up of his holdings to be quite different from the small saver's. The basic forms of saving account for only £1 in every eight, whilst nearly £2 in every three is in stocks and shares.

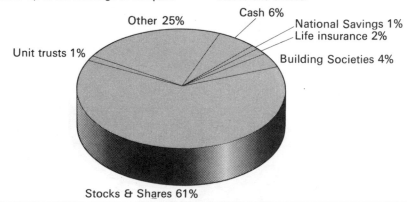

Other 25%
Cash 6%
National Savings 1%
Life insurance 2%
Unit trusts 1%
Building Societies 4%
Stocks & Shares 61%

DOES THE STOCK MARKET MATTER?

■ What percentage of company financial needs was provided by the issue of shares on the stock exchange in 1973? Was it:
  (i) over 90%?
  (II) around 50%?
  (iii) less than 10%?
■ Issues of new ordinary shares provided only 0.7%, with another 0.4% from preference shares and debentures. Thus only just over £1 of every £100 that companies needed to raise came from the stock market. In only one year out of the last eight has the market provided more than 5% of industry's financial needs.

■ So where does industry get its money from?
■ Mostly it comes from companies' own retained profits which are ploughed back into the firm. Companies tend to do their *own* saving.

■ What then is the importance of the stock market?
■ It plays a key role in issuing government bonds, since so much public spending is financed by government borrowing.
■ It provides a mechanism for shifting savings around as people and institutions continually buy, sell, re-buy and re-sell shares.
■ It finances over half of total company spending on take-overs. In 1972 58% of the cost of mergers and acquisitions was met by the issue of ordinary shares and not by cash.
■ Finally, it is both a reflection of, and an influence upon, the state of confidence in industry. This is a key factor in investment decisions by businessmen.

OUR SAVINGS DO MATTER BECAUSE THEY ALLOW MORE INVESTMENT IN FACTORIES AND MACHINES WHICH HELPS TO RAISE FUTURE LIVING STANDARDS.

Governments have not allowed savings to be eaten away by inflation because they think they are unimportant. On the contrary, they (and economists) have been at pains to stress the benefits to the economy of still more saving. And they are right.

Savings are very significant in the national economy because they result from decisions to consume less than our incomes would allow us to. And these decisions not to consume enable part of the nation's resources to be diverted into investment—the production of capital goods like factories and machines. Savings, if they are channelled into productive investment, make it possible to produce a greater output of goods and services for consumption in the future.

Of course, everything depends on whether savings do find their way into productive investment. In some cases, as for example with a farmer, it is the saver who then *himself* invests in a new tractor, barn or land improvement. However, most of our personal savings are handled by financial intermediaries like banks, building societies, pension and insurance funds. *We* have little control on whether our savings go towards modernising British industry or finish up financing property speculation.

The fact remains that a further reason why the personal saver should feel cheated is that he is entitled not only to protection against inflation but also to some positive reward—since one of the reasons why the economy has grown richer over the years is *because* he was prepared to forgo some immediate consumption.

There are three main reasons why governments have largely ignored the damage which inflation inflicts on personal savers.
■ Although personal saving is important, two-thirds of the total saving in the economy is done, not by individuals and families, but by companies in the form of ploughed-back profits.
■ So far, inflation has not reduced the incentive to save. Surprisingly, we have been saving an increasing proportion of our incomes over the years. Partly this may be due to savers being unaware of just how badly they are penalised by inflation; but is also because they lack any alternative and have to make do with the best of a bad lot when it comes to choosing between different ways of saving.

Why have governments neglected savers?

WHO SAVED WHAT IN 1973?
Out of every £100 saved in 1973:
£52 was by companies
£36 was by individuals
£12 was by the public sector.

41

THE SAVINGS RATIO
(Savings as % of take-
home pay)
1968 7.9%
1969 8.1%
1970 9.0%
1971 9.0%
1972 9.6%
1973 10.5%

PUBLIC SECTOR
BORROWING
REQUIREMENT
(£m)
1971 1,400
1972 2,100
1973 4,200
1974 7,600
1975 (budget forecast)
      9,100

■ Since governments are themselves very large borrowers, the lower that interest rates are, the less they have to pay out in interest payments.

This is not to suggest that governments have therefore deliberately engineered inflation. It is not even to blame them particularly for their failure to stop prices from rising: as we have seen, economists can offer no clear explanations of inflation or solutions. But it does raise the question of whether governments should not therefore have accepted more responsibility than they have for compensating those who save and lose in process of doing so.

One way of protecting savers is by tying interest rates to increases in the cost of living according to the principle of *indexation.* What this means is that if you save £100 for a year and that during the year prices rise by 20%, then you will receive back £120 plus some element of real interest. In fact, in 1975 the government did take a small initiative in this direction by introducing two index-linked savings schemes—one for those over retirement age and the other on a save-as-you-earn basis. But why doesn't the government set a good example by applying the same principle of indexation to all of its own borrowing? Such a policy would have far-reaching effects.

If lending to the government was made inflation-proof, then other forms of saving would become very unattractive. The building societies, for example, would have great difficulty in persuading people to deposit with them unless they followed suit and indexed *their* borrowing rates. With inflation at 20%, it would mean that building societies would have to offer something like 23%— and charge those who have mortgages from them a rate even higher than this.

INDEX-LINKED SCHEMES
Save-As-You-Earn scheme
A regular monthly saving of between £4 and £20. This is repayable after 5 years after your contributions have been revalued according to the Retail Price Index. This means that you are repaid the same amount in *real* terms as you have contributed. Your savings are therefore guaranteed.

Retirement Issue of National Savings Certificates
People over retirement age can buy between £10 and £500 worth of certificates, which are repayable after 5 years with the purchase price revalued according to the Retail Price Index. The same real amount is again therefore repayable, along with a special bonus of 4% of the purchase price.

This would mean roughly a doubling of mortgage repayments. For most people this would impose an impossible burden and would exclude them from the possibility of house ownership. However, a way of avoiding this happening has been proposed by Professor Michael Parkin of Manchester University. He suggests that mortgages should be repaid on a quite different basis from the present one.

INDEXED MORTGAGES
The figures below compare existing arrangements for repaying a £2,000 mortgage over 25 years with the Parkin approach based on a real rate of interest of 4%. The figures assume that the 1974 inflation rate of 20% continues over the life of the mortgage.

| Year of mortgage | Borrower's likely income | Annual repayment | |
		Present arrangements	Parkin approach
first year	£1,000	£240	£150
tenth year	£5,000	£240	£800
twenty-fifth year	£80,000	£240	£12,000

With inflation at 20% matched by the rise in the borrower's income, repayments under existing arrangements begin as 24% of income and fall eventually to only 0.3% of income in the final year.
Under the Parkin proposals repayments stay at about 15% of income throughout. There is thus no increase in the burden of repayments, whilst building societies would be able to offer their savers a real rate of return.

This proposal exposes both a fundamental conflict of interest and an important moral issue. Despite the fact that the new system might mean lower repayments during the early years of a mortgage, it certainly won't commend itself either to those who are at present paying for their own homes or who plan to do so in the future. What now happens is that those who borrow from building societies do very well out of inflation, as their repayments fall to quite small proportions of their incomes; but they do so at the expense of the savers who provide the building societies with their funds. Morally, it seems only right that it is the saver who should be protected against inflation; but since there are 5 million people in this country buying their own homes, it will be a brave government which introduces indexation and brings about a major redistribution in favour of savers (rather than, as at present, further encouraging borrowers by granting them tax allowances).

Moreover, a further implication of indexation would be the greatly increased cost of the government's own borrowing. For example, if it now borrows £1,000 million at a 10% interest rate, then the annual cost of servicing this debt is £100 million. If it were to bring its interest rate into line with a rate of inflation of 20%, the annual cost would rise to £200 million. This difference of £100 million is the amount of extra revenue which the government would have to raise if it did not benefit from a low interest rate. Bearing in mind that in 1975 the government's borrowing requirement was of the order of £9,000 million, it can be seen just how substantially higher taxes might have to be if index-linked government borrowing were to be introduced.

Higher taxes based on the ability to pay. Bigger mortgage repayments for those who want, and can afford to own their own houses. These are part of the politically unpopular price which might have to be paid if we are to protect savers rather than as at present let them bear the burden of inflation to the advantage of those who borrow.

A MORAL TALE

In 1950 Mr S. decided to start saving on a regular basis in order to buy a house in 1975 upon his retirement.

In 1950 also Mr B. took out a mortgage for 25 years to buy a house.

Which of them will have done best, and what kind of advantages will he have had over the other?

Mr B. will undoubtedly have had all the advantages:

- He will have bought his house at the 1950 price, and now it is his own at the 1975 value.
- He will have been paying smaller and smaller real amounts back to the building society.
- These repayments will also have been smaller and smaller proportions of his own income.
- He will have enjoyed the tax relief on his mortgage interest.

By contrast, Mr S. will not have had any of these advantages, and will also have suffered from the continual erosion of the value of his savings by inflation over the years. To keep up with inflation Mr S. would have had to part with a larger proportion of his spendable income over the period than Mr B., even though the latter was paying interest on his loan as well as repayments. Perhaps the moral of this story is really whether people like you find the moral acceptable!

THE IMPORTANCE OF IMPORTING

'The announcement yesterday of a sharp reduction in the U.K.'s overseas trade deficit brought relief to the foreign exchange markets at the end of a difficult week for the pound.'

Once a month headlines like this bombard us. Sometimes optimistic, sometimes pessimistic, but always based on the assumption that the trade gap and the state of the £ are important enough to us to justify the thick black print of the headline or the grave voice of the TV newscaster. But how important is foreign trade in our everyday lives? Well, just think for a moment about the number of imported goods and materials you use or consume in the first hour of your day. The following are just some of the things which may well have come from abroad, or been made from foreign materials:

■ *alarm clock, tea, sugar, butter, clothes, radio, electric shaver or razor blade, soap and towel, petrol for your journey to work, and perhaps your car too.*

A second look at the list brings a key distinction to light.

■ With some of the items it is absolutely necessary that we import them, since we can't produce them here.

■ But with others we are choosing to buy from abroad rather than using the British alternative.

What are the implications for our balance of payments position and for government policies?

This chapter considers how realistic and how effective is the *Buy British* slogan.

For every two pounds that we spend on British goods and services, we spend one on imports from abroad. Isn't this rather too much to put into the pockets of foreigners? After all, foreign competition threatens British jobs. Moreover, since one post-war government after another has used the balance of payments as a stick to beat us with—the reason for higher taxes, the need to work harder and for general belt-tightening—then why don't we go for the obvious solution: buy British and get the balance of payments off our backs once and for all?

Nobody would argue that Britain should try to be completely self-sufficent. Over 40% of our imports are foodstuffs and raw materials which either we can't produce ourselves or could do so only very expensively by creating artificially conditions which exist naturally in other parts of the world. One basic reason why nations trade with each other is because natural resources are unevenly distributed between different countries.

Why nations trade

But the other 60% of our imports are made up of manufactured or processed goods which could have been produced in the United Kingdom. German cameras, Japanese cars and television sets, transistors from Hong Kong, shirts from Portugal, washing machines from Italy—why do we import all these things which British manufacturers and workers could profitably be employed in producing?

The economist's answer is that international trade enables us to obtain goods more *cheaply*. Specialising in those goods which we can produce most efficiently and then exporting them is a cheaper way of getting hold of other goods than making them ourselves.

The basis on which countries should specialise is that of *comparative* advantage. Benefits from international trade don't only arise because different nations can produce particular goods *absolutely* more cheaply than others. Even in the case where one country can produce everything more cheaply than another, it will still pay it to concentrate on those lines of production in which its superiority is the greatest; by then exporting those goods it will be able to get supplies of others more cheaply in terms of the resources it uses than if it had produced them itself. A doctor may be better at both medicine and typing than his secretary, but it still pays him to specialise in medicine and employ the secretary to do his typing.

Paradoxically, the whole point of embarking on international trade is to destroy certain of our own industries. The aim is to cut back on inefficient types of production and to shift the resources used there into more productive employment. However, this makes sense only if two assumptions underlying the economist's theory of international trade hold good.

■ Full employment. There's no point in making *further* resources unemployed when there are empty factories and unemployed workers already available for productive use.

■ Labour and capital are mobile. Allowing, for example, Lancashire textile workers to be made redundant by foreign competition only improves the efficiency of the economy if they are then re-absorbed in more productive occupations. That depends on how easy it is to induce new industries to move into the area or for the workers to find fresh employment elsewhere. In practice, labour and capital have often proved to be very immobile.

None the less, we are undoubtedly much better off with international trade than without it—in the same way that families, if they tried to be self-sufficient, would find themselves materially very poor. Specialisation has been the key to the increased affluence of the past few centuries, and international trade simply extends the principle to a world scale. But the fact that there are substantial benefits to be had from international trade does not mean that we should therefore aim at maximising it. There are the difficulties just mentioned; and, after a certain point, the gains from further trade become trifling compared with the payments problems which, in the British case, have so often accompanied them.

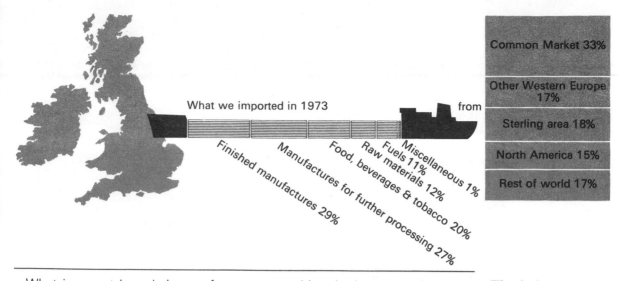

What we imported in 1973 from

Finished manufactures 29%
Manufactures for further processing 27%
Food, beverages & tobacco 20%
Raw materials 12%
Fuels 11%
Miscellaneous 1%

Common Market 33%
Other Western Europe 17%
Sterling area 18%
North America 15%
Rest of world 17%

**The balance
of payments**

What is meant by a balance of payments problem is that we can't lay our hands on sufficient gold and foreign exchange (dollars, marks, yen, francs) to pay for what we want to do: to import goods and services, have foreign holidays, maintain bases overseas, aid underdeveloped countries and invest in foreign businesses. That has more often than not been the British predicament during the postwar period.

These currencies in which foreigners naturally demand to be paid when they sell to us can only be obtained in one of two ways. We can either earn them—or we can borrow them.

**How much do we
earn?**

In 1971, by exporting nearly 30% of our national output—machinery, cars and lorries, chemicals, textiles, whisky and so on—we earned £8,800 million. That was rather more than we needed to pay for our imports of foodstuffs, raw materials and manufactured goods. But 1971 happened to be one of a very few exceptional years in which earnings from merchandise exports turned out to be sufficient to finance merchandise imports.

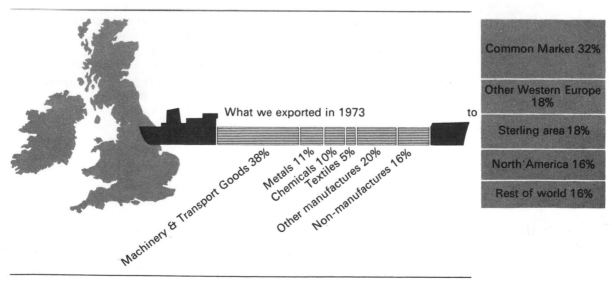

What we exported in 1973 to

Machinery & Transport Goods 38%
Metals 11%
Chemicals 10%
Textiles 5%
Other manufactures 20%
Non-manufactures 16%

Common Market 32%
Other Western Europe 18%
Sterling area 18%
North America 16%
Rest of world 16%

Throughout our economic history, the 'trade figures' have nearly always been bad—there's nothing new about that at all. Before the war, exports of goods used to pay for only about two-thirds of our imports of goods. The postwar years saw a dramatic narrowing of this 'trade gap' only for it to be widened again by the recent increase in oil prices.

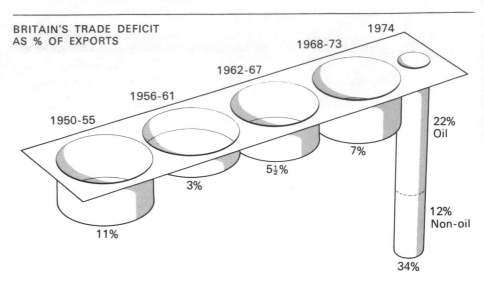

BRITAIN'S TRADE DEFICIT
AS % OF EXPORTS

1950-55 — 11%
1956-61 — 3%
1962-67 — 5½%
1968-73 — 7%
1974 — 22% Oil, 12% Non-oil, 34%

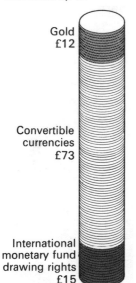

In 1974, each £100 worth of reserves was made up of

Gold £12

Convertible currencies £73

International monetary fund drawing rights £15

How much are we borrowing ?

These are the figures which month after month the news media gravely announce as fresh evidence of impending national disaster ; but in fact there is another important source of foreign exchange earnings apart from trading in goods. 'Invisible' exports arise from payments by foreigners to U.K. residents for a variety of services—like travelling on a British ship or airline, using British banks, insurance or commodity markets, or having a holiday in Britain. In addition, there is a flow of profits, interest and dividends on past British investments overseas.

These invisible earnings have always been substantially greater than the amount that we spend on similar items. Sometimes they have been enough to more than offset the visible trade deficit and yield a favourable 'balance of payments on current account'. Recently, they have not.

A deficit on the current balance of payments, spending more on goods and services than we earn, has the same implications for a nation as it does for individuals and families. Those who have sold to us want paying, and we can only pay them by either drawing on our past saving—or by borrowing.

First of all, the nation's 'past savings' in this respect are made up of reserves of gold and foreign exchange which have been accumulated from previous earnings and are held by the Bank of England. Recently, these have been hovering around the £3,000 million mark. That may sound a lot, but they would soon be eaten up if they were used to finance current account deficits as large as those of the past few years.

As for borrowing, foreigners are only prepared to lend to us when it pays them to do so, and for so long as they think we are creditworthy. One way in which they do so is by holding British bank balances or central or local authority bonds. Partly this may be a matter of convenience for them because sterling is a

BRITAIN'S BALANCE OF PAYMENTS

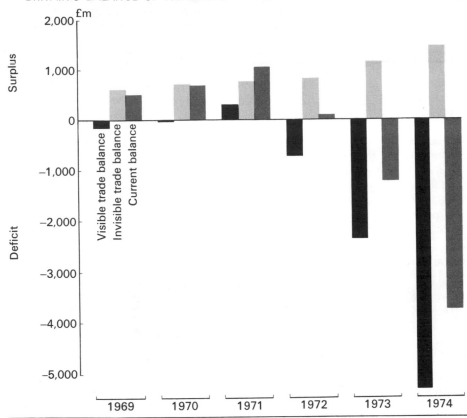

currency in which debts between other countries are sometimes settled. Generally, however, their willingness to lend to us depends on:
■ How high British interest rates are compared to those in other international financial centres.
■ What they think is going to happen to the external value of the pound—the exchange rate. If they think that the pound is going to weaken, then part of their interest earnings will be wiped out by the fact that their sterling holdings will buy less foreign currency.

There is another important form of borrowing from overseas. When foreign companies decide to set up subsidiaries in Britain or to buy up British firms, they have to transfer the equivalent amount of their own currencies to acquire the necessary amount of sterling. In effect, they are lending us foreign exchange on a long-term basis. Once again, they only do so if they see the prospect of a profitable rate of return on their capital. Since British firms may similarly be investing overseas (and there is also an outflow of capital on government account—for example, to finance foreign aid), the impact on the balance of payments depends on which of the two flows is the greater.

Finally, Britain has frequently resorted to 'official financing'. This means either using our drawing rights at the International Monetary Fund or persuading other governments to lend a helping hand.

In 1973, net borrowing from abroad totalled nearly £1,500 million—almost £30 per head for every man, woman and child in this country. Since borrowing

Is it wise to borrow?

49

WE'RE PUTTING THE COUNTRY IN HOCK—HEADING FOR NATIONAL BANKRUPTCY.

BALANCE OF PAYMENT BRITAIN GETS MASSIVE LOAN

stores up future trouble for the balance of payments in that we shall have to pay foreigners interest every year on their loans and investments, it only makes sense to borrow on such a scale if the current account deficit is thought to be temporary and/or if the borrowing is used to finance projects which will increase our future international competitiveness—and therefore, in the long run, pay for itself.

It is the hope that Britain will wipe out its oil deficit through the exploitation of the North Sea deposits which has been put forward as the main justification of present borrowing. However, critics have suggested that we shall have cause for regret in the future because far too little of it has been channelled into productive investment. Instead, we have used foreign borrowing to sustain consumption at the level to which we have become accustomed.

However, it is worth bearing in mind that despite the recent heavy inflow of capital, our overseas investment over the years means that we still own substantially more foreign assets than do foreigners in this country. In other words, contrary to what seems to be the popular impression, Britain remains an international *creditor* nation.

BRITAIN'S BALANCE SHEET
(end 1973 position)

	£m.
TOTAL U.K. ASSETS	£63,075
TOTAL U.K. LIABILITIES	£59,600

Who's worried about the balance of payments?

The balance of payments does matter because it affects those things about which all are most concerned—job security, prices and our standard of living.

■ JOBS may be at stake because one of the ways in which governments have tried to cope with the balance of payments is by applying deflationary measures—running the economy at less than full stretch to avoid more imports being sucked in.

■ PRICES soar to the extent that the payments problem results from the increased cost of basic commodities, as has been the case recently.

■ STANDARDS OF LIVING are threatened. Governments may be deterred from pushing for faster growth by the fear that it will cause an unmanageable flood of imports; and prospects for future improvements in living standards are marred by the need to repay the heavy foreign debts which we are now incurring. There are those who argue that we should face up to the problem now rather than postpone it by borrowing, and accept the cut of 5-6% in our present consumption levels which would be needed if we were to live within our immediate means.

What can be done?

An obvious solution to our balance of payments difficulties seems that governments should do everything to encourage a policy of Buying British, and to back it up by imposing controls on the amount that can be imported. After all, when the oil deficit has been eliminated, the remaining discrepancy between imports and exports will only amount to a few per cent of national output. Surely the easiest way of coping with the problem is to say NO to the relatively small quantity of imports which make all the difference—either by setting *quotas* on the amount of imports allowed or by erecting *tariffs* which make them unattractively expensive.

There are three main problems about this approach.

■ British consumers would suffer by being forced to buy British goods which were either dearer or which they regarded as inferior. They would also have less variety of choice. Many foreign goods are bought, not because they are cheaper or better but simply because they are different. But, would some restriction on consumer choice be worth an easing of the balance of payments difficulty?

■ Protection from foreign competition might make British producers still less efficient than they are now. Once again, it would be the consumer who would have to bear the cost. Exports, too, might suffer if feather-bedding of domestic producers reduced their international competitiveness.

■ How would those who sell to us react to a restriction of their market? Their earnings would fall—which might mean that they could buy less from us. There is the further possibility that they would retaliate by imposing similar controls on our exports to them.

In any case, with our enmeshment with Europe and as signatories to international agreements like GATT (the General Agreement on Tariffs and Trade), it would be difficult for us to introduce import controls without general consent. Those with whom we trade might be persuaded by the argument that a small reduction in their exports to us now will pay off later. Freed from the balance of payments constraint, British governments could push for faster growth which would subsequently mean much larger markets for foreigners.

But if the dangers of a policy of Buying British are thought to be too great or politically unacceptable, then what are the alternatives? The balance of payments will have to be tackled *either* by a modernisation of British industry and control of inflation to make us more internationally competitive *or* we will have to accept the implications of a consistently falling overseas value of the pound. These are matters which form part of the content of the next chapter.

A TWO-WAY RELATIONSHIP

The chart below shows the level of unemployment in recent years. Each 'D' denotes that there was a serious balance of payments deficit in that year. There seem to be two patterns:
■ the deficits usually follow periods of falling unemployment, and
■ periods of rising unemployment normally follow deficits.
Can you suggest reasons for each of these?
■ Unemployment tends to rise after a deficit as a result of tough deflationary measures introduced by the government. The intention is to reduce consumer spending at home in order to cut down on imports and so encourage British industry to try to sell abroad.
■ A balance of payments deficit following a period of falling unemployment suggests that the economy has been working flat out, and that, as a result, imports are sucked in as home production soars and people spend their extra pay, and goods which were destined for export markets get diverted to home sales.

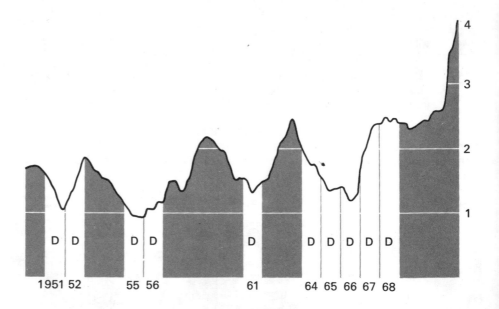

KEEPING UP WITH THE SCHMIDTS

SOME STARK TRUTHS FOR BRITAIN

'The real economic condition of Britain is one of diminishing competitiveness, deteriorating balance of payments and declining standards of living. Until very recently this economic and social decline had not been so marked. Britain had been growing, but more slowly than other countries. Yet in 1974, for the first time in the postwar era, Britain's individual wealth registered an absolute decline and it is almost certain that this will continue as a long-range absolute decline. Unless heroic efforts are made on a national scale there will be many such years—intermittent but frequent—an insidious and protracted process of shrinking real national income and personal welfare. This is a perilous situation, and all the more so because Britain as a whole refuses to face the facts.'

The researchers of the Hudson Institute who came to the above conclusions in their 1974 Report (The U.K. in 1980, Associated Business Programmes) certainly gave us a lot of stick. They in turn have been attacked strongly for their troubles. How near the mark were they?

How many of the viewpoints expressed in the above extract do you find yourself in agreement with?

On what kind of evidence are your own attitudes based?

This chapter looks at whether Britain really is in decline, and tries to identify the kind of policies which are now necessary if we are to avoid the possibility of a similar Hudson Report in a decade's time.

We are constantly being warned that if things go on as they are, then Britain will soon become the poor man of Europe. The prophets of doom paint a picture of a once great industrial nation reverting to semi-industrial poverty—with declining living standards and the status which we used to attach to countries like Italy and Spain.

For those who take their holidays abroad, this does seem to be the writing on the wall. Year by year, as the pound becomes worth less in terms of other currencies, the British tourist is made aware that it is he who is doing the pinching and scraping while those from other countries seem to be coping much better. It is not just that everything is so much more expensive there than here—there's little change from a pound after buying a couple of cups of coffee. It is the fact that while *we* worry about how dear everything is, the Germans and the French and the Dutch can apparently afford to enjoy themselves none the less.

Since this wasn't always the case, doesn't it mean that we are becoming poorer and will either have to learn to live with it—or do something about it?

Whether it feels like it or not, and this is one of those areas in which memories tend to be short-lived, we have in fact become substantially richer over the postwar period. Admittedly, much of the rise which has taken place in money incomes has been offset by inflation. But even after allowing for rising prices, real income per head in Britain has roughly doubled since the war. That doubling

Are we getting poorer?

has been made possible by the growth of the economy's capacity to produce goods and services, a growth rate which has frequently been decried as 'only' about 2½% a year. Although these national statistics tell us nothing about *what* extra output is being produced and *who* is getting the extra income, there are other figures which support the view that our living standards have greatly improved.

Consumers' Expenditure (*1970 prices*)

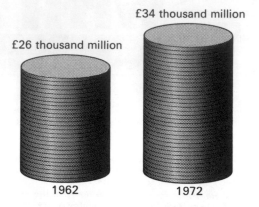

£34 thousand million

£26 thousand million

1962   1972

■ Private consumption in real terms rose by nearly a third in the decade 1962-1972.

■ Expenditure on social services—which are as much a part of our living standards as private spending—has risen at the same rate as the growth of national income as a whole.

Current Expenditure on Social Services as % of National Income

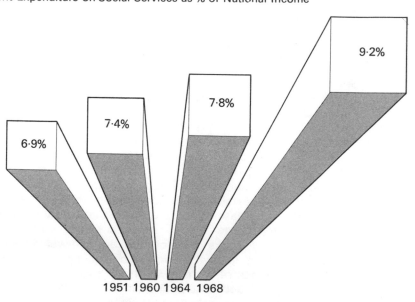

6·9%   7·4%   7·8%   9·2%

1951 1960 1964 1968

The idea that we are getting worse off is simply wrong. But what has been happening is that Britain has been getting richer at a slower rate than many other countries. While getting absolutely richer, we have become *relatively* poorer.

It is notoriously difficult to make accurate international comparisons of living standards. They depend on what period is chosen; economic information in different countries is not always put together on the same basis; and there is the problem of translating figures expressed in one currency into those of another. Statistics like these, as the debate on British membership of the EEC showed, can be manipulated to support quite different versions of the truth.

But there still can't be much doubt that, in material terms, Britain *has* slipped behind in the race for higher living standards.

■ Britain has had a lower rate of economic growth than most of the other industrial nations—and this is true for pretty well any period which is taken during the postwar years.

■ Private consumption in the U.K. has grown more slowly in recent years.

■ Britain has also lagged in the rate at which social spending has been increasing.

MY, HOW YOU'VE NOT GROWN

Average annual rates of growth (at constant prices) 1961-1971

	Total	Per head
U.K.	2.7%	2.2%
Belgium	4.9%	4.3%
France	5.8%	4.7%
Germany	4.6%	3.7%
Italy	4.9%	4.2%
Netherlands	5.4%	4.1%
Japan	10.2%	9.0%
USA	4.1%	2.9%

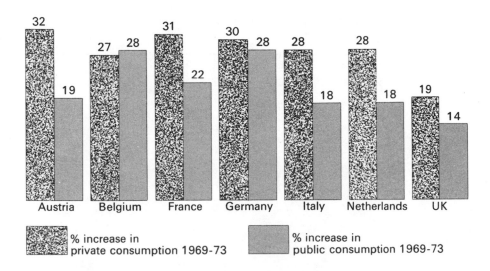

% increase in private consumption 1969-73

% increase in public consumption 1969-73

One significant and ominous international comparison which can be made is about the proportion of total output which different nations use for immediate consumption rather than to make investment goods (like factories and machines) which can help to increase the future productive capacity of the economy. Britain's record in this respect is of taking a markedly higher slice of national output for present consumption and of devoting far less to investment than other countries. To the extent that we have managed to keep up with the Schmidts at all, has it been only by neglecting the build-up of capital which is needed for improvements in future living standards?

Certainly, it is not more investment as such which is the key to faster economic growth. What counts is that the investment is *productive*. But British investment has either not been enough or its quality has been inferior because its results as measured by how much output per man is produced have been relatively disappointing. The productivity figures suggest that the British worker (whatever

his own faults) also labours under the handicap of having to work with a smaller quantity and less up-to-date machinery than Mr Schmidt.

A second way in which Britain has been doing less well than others is in containing inflation. This is true of both the past few decades and also of those recent years in which, although they were all caught in the prices explosion, most countries have been far more successful in bringing inflation down within tolerable limits again.

INVESTMENT AS % OF NATIONAL INCOME, 1966-1967

USA	17
U.K.	18
Germany	22
France	23
Netherlands	27
Norway	31

In 1971 investment for each workers in British manufacturing industry was less than half that in France, Japan or the USA, and well below that in Germany or Italy.

OUTPUT PER EMPLOYEE 1961-1971

	Annual average % increase
U.K.	2.8
Belgium	4.0
France	5.0
Germany	4.4
Italy	5.4
Netherlands	4.4
Japan	8.8
USA	2.2

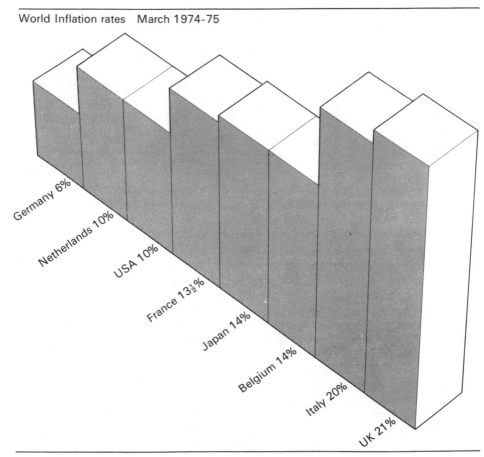

World Inflation rates   March 1974-75

Germany 6%
Netherlands 10%
USA 10%
France 13½%
Japan 14%
Belgium 14%
Italy 20%
UK 21%

Thirdly, many of the European economies and Japan have enjoyed a virtuous circle of high investment → greater productivity → more international competitiveness → strong balance of payments → the freedom to push for faster growth and hence higher investment. Britain, on the other hand, has found it impossible to break out of a vicious circle of low investment → low growth → balance of payments difficulties → the need to hold back expansion to prevent them getting worse.

One of the major symptoms of Britain's relative economic weakness has been the falling pound. In June 1972 a pound would have bought 12.1 French francs, 7.7 deutschmarks, or 2.4 dollars. Three years later, the amount of foreign currencies which could be bought for a pound has been cut by over a quarter. Before asking why this has happened and what it means, we first have to see what determines the price of one currency in terms of another.

The price of the pound, the external value of the pound, depends on how many pounds are being bought and sold in the foreign exchange market. Those *buying* pounds (and paying for them with foreign currencies) will be foreigners who want them

■ to pay their bills from exporters of British goods and services
■ to buy British stocks or shares or companies
■ to hold in British bank accounts, possibly because they expect that the value of the pound is going to rise in the future or to earn interest.

Those *selling* pounds (to buy foreign currencies) will be those engaged in similar trading, capital or speculative transactions in the opposite direction.

If the number of pounds people wish to sell exceeds the number which others want to buy, then the market price of the pound falls. However, until 1972, this was prevented from happening by the Bank of England which would step in and itself increase the demand for pounds—by selling some foreign exchange from the nation's reserves. In this way, exchange rates were kept stable by Britain and other leading world traders under an agreement with the International Monetary Fund. Occasional upward or downward adjustments were then termed devaluation or revaluation.

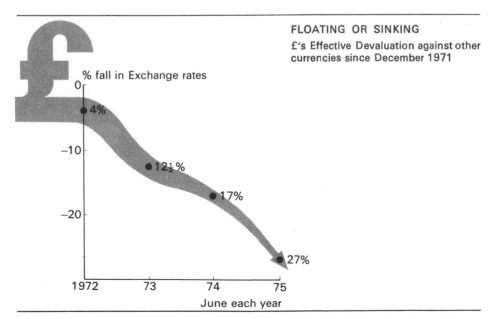

FLOATING OR SINKING
£'s Effective Devaluation against other currencies since December 1971

% fall in Exchange rates
0
● 4%
−10
● 12½%
● 17%
−20
● 27%
1972   73   74   75
June each year

Why the pound has fallen

However, in June 1972, it was decided to let the pound temporarily 'float' and find its own level; it has subsequently floated downwards by over 25%. The reasons for this depreciation are not difficult to find.

■ The higher rate of British inflation. With stable exchange rates, our exports would have become increasingly expensive and imports relatively cheaper. We would have sold less abroad and bought more imports. The consequent balance of payments deficit could only have been met by decimating our already small foreign exchange reserves. A floating rate of exchange, on the other hand, has enabled British selling prices overseas to be kept in line with others. The falling pound offsets the relatively higher rate of British inflation, but it also meant that the cost of our imports has continued to soar.

■ Non-price factors have also contributed to the balance of payments weakness which has caused the falling pound. Some economists have argued that we sell the wrong products, or that we sell to the wrong markets—or that we're simply not good enough at selling and keeping to delivery dates.

'It should be remembered that the impressive penetration of world markets achieved by the Japanese owes a good deal to the dramatic changes in the structure of their production and trade towards the fast growing products and a major improvement in technical competence.'
(NEDO Study by M. Panic and A. H. Rajan, 1971)

'We recommend that British Leyland should devote more effort than in the past to developing overseas sales. In recent years BL has had a poor reputation in many overseas markets for not keeping delivery promises, for shortage of parts, and for inadequate after-sales service.'
(Ryder Report on British Leyland, 1975)

■ Speculative pressure has at times played a part. If people think that the pound is going to fall further—then they will sell pounds and, in the process, depress the value of the pound proving themselves right.

Finally, of course, the pound would have fallen to still lower levels as a result of the oil deficit in the balance of payments had that not been largely offset by the fact that foreigners, largely the oil countries themselves lent Britain large sums as 1974/5 (for which purpose they buy pounds).

Does the falling pound matter to *you*—apart from making your foreign holiday pricier? It certainly does. It means that import prices are continuously pushed up, and since imports are important items in both consumer budgets and the costs of manufacturing, a further twist is given to the inflationary spiral. The falling pound is partly caused by our higher inflation—and our higher inflation is, in turn, partly caused by the falling pound. Secondly, to repeat the point already made, the falling pound is a symptom of our relative inefficiency—of the extent to which we are falling behind.

What can be done?

Can the slide be halted? Can something be done to prevent Britain's relative economic decline? Judging by our past record, the prospects are not very hopeful. What is needed is:

■ A shift of a substantial quantity of resources into the investment sector of the economy—to re-equip British industry and make it capable of competing more effectively in both home and overseas markets.

■ To make that shift at the right time—to ensure that when world trade begins to boom, the British economy is poised to take advantage of it.

In neither of these respects have British governments been very successful in the past. At times, they have released resources (i.e. allowed unemployment to rise) but they have then failed to see that they were subsequently redeployed in more productive uses. And secondly, when we have come out of recessions, investment has only picked up *after* domestic consumption has begun to boom and take up resources which should have gone into investment.

The solution may therefore have to lie in more radical restructuring policies aimed at improving productivity and getting the timing of investment right—by, for example, offering direct inducements to companies to undertake investment during recessionary phases. These are matters which we shall return to in the final chapter.

But perhaps we don't want to keep up with the Schmidts anyway? Why bother about slipping behind, particularly when most of us are secretly convinced that ours is a more pleasant and civilised way of life?

The obsession with getting richer by maximising the rate of economic growth has rightly been criticised in recent years for neglecting to ask—growth of *what* and for *whom* and at what *cost*? But it is rather difficult to believe that the British people have implicitly opted out of the growth race and settled for a tranquil stagnancy. Then there are so many problems—like raising the present standards of housing, education and health, and narrowing the gap between the rich and the poor nations of the world—which further material growth could help to solve (as well as redistributing what we have already). What is important is that growth takes the right form and that the quality of life is not sacrificed in achieving it.

It is even doubtful whether opting out is viable for a small island economy heavily dependent on and enmeshed in the international economy. A policy of no-growth might imply a cumulative *fall* in our living standards—as investment is diverted elsewhere and British products become decreasingly attractive. Sad though it may be to some, staying as we are today is not a real alternative to keeping up with the Schmidts.

CHECKING FOR FAULTS
In the same way as a car mechanic looks for signs of bad performance and possible causes of danger, the economist should be able to draw up a checklist of similar signs of the health of the economy. Taking this chapter as your guide, what would be your checklist of points requiring attention in the U.K.'s economic performance?

Here is a suggested summary:
Low growth
(leading to slow rise in private consumption and slow rise in social spending).
Low investment
Low productivity (output per employee)
High inflation
Poor international competitiveness
Weak currency

PLAYING THE CHANCELLOR'S GAME

SPARE A THOUGHT FOR THE CHANCELLOR. THE BUDGET IS A VERY IMPORTANT WEAPON FOR REGULATING THE GENERAL ECONOMIC SITUATION—

AND IT'S A DIFFICULT ONE TO WIELD.

After Denis Healey's Budget of April 1975 you were faced with:
■ a higher rate of income tax
■ a higher rate of value added tax on many goods
■ higher duties on tobacco and drink
■ higher vehicle excise duties (car tax).
These are the things that probably affected you most directly as the Chancellor tried to collect an extra £1,200 million in tax revenue. To what extent did you accept that the economic position at the time justified you being penalised in these ways? What objectives was the budget trying to achieve? Were there better ways of trying to achieve them? Or fairer ways?

The budget is the sharpest focus in the year for bringing your personal position into line with the nation's overall economic position. This chapter looks at the nature and background of the budget and at the factors which decide whether Chancellors present us with good news or bad from that battered old red despatch box.

The contents of the Chancellor's red despatch box on Budget day still rivet the nation's attention—because a whole variety of our personal decisions depend on what he has to say. Will easier hire purchase make it possible for you to replace your old car? Will the taxman be grabbing an even larger slice of your paypacket? Is the weekly trip to the supermarket going to become even more alarmingly expensive? While the pundits drone on about the technical niceties of the Budget and its wider implications, it is these much more basic considerations which interest the majority of us.

Yet the pundits are right. Our everyday lives are likely to be affected far more by the general economic impact of the Budget than by its particular items which seem of most immediate concern to us—because the Budget is one of the main instruments by which governments try to influence the number of people who are in work, the price level and the rate of expansion of the economy. The Budget is not simply the means by which the Chancellor raises enough tax revenue to finance government spending. It is an attempt to coordinate a multitude of incompatible decisions and to compromise between conflicting interests in the economy—so that it is steered towards the achievement of national economic objectives.

The object of the Chancellor's game

At the most basic level, the problem which the Chancellor seeks to solve is how to secure an appropriate balance between *output* and *spending*.

If all the resources in the economy are actively engaged in production, they will be capable of creating a certain value of *full employment output*.

If the economy is to run at that level of full employment output, then there must be enough spending to buy all the goods and services produced; but how much in fact is spent is the result of innumerable decisions—by consumers, firms, exporters and importers, and the government.

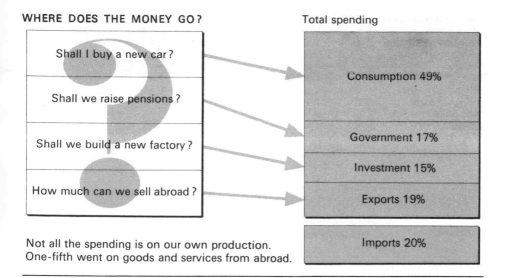

WHERE DOES THE MONEY GO?

Shall I buy a new car?

Shall we raise pensions?

Shall we build a new factory?

How much can we sell abroad?

Not all the spending is on our own production.
One-fifth went on goods and services from abroad.

Total spending

Consumption 49%

Government 17%

Investment 15%

Exports 19%

Imports 20%

It is obviously improbable in the extreme that all these individual spending decisions should by chance add up to a total amount which is just sufficient, no more and no less, to buy the full employment output.

■ If spending is less than the value of full employment output, then some goods will be unsold. Producers will plan to reduce output, the economy will head for a recession, and unemployment will emerge. The shortfall of spending below full employment is called *the deflationary gap.*

■ If spending is greater than the value of full employment output, then there will be shortages of goods which will lead to higher prices. The amount by which spending exceeds the value of full employment output is called *the inflationary gap.*

Chancellors generally aim at avoiding both of these situations by keeping the level of spending in the economy on the razor's edge between unemployment and inflation. In looking after the nation's economic health, the Chancellor must diagnose, prescribe, treat—and, hopefully, bring off a cure. These are the stages involved in the preparation, presentation and execution of his Budget proposals.

In diagnosing the condition of the economy, the Chancellor first of all has to decide what its present state is, and then to forecast what will happen to it if he sits back and does nothing. In making his diagnosis, he has the benefit of a mass of official economic data (the result of all that form-filling about which most of us complain)—and the services of the Treasury economic and statistical advisers.

Diagnosis

Unfortunately, both the information and the experts have severe limitations.

■ The figures may be out-of-date, referring to a situation some months ago which has already changed. They are also subject to a considerable margin of error. The Chancellor may therefore be uncertain even about where the economy is now.

■ When it comes to forecasting developments over the next twelve or eighteen months, his problems are even more acute. Given the present state of economic knowledge and the inherent difficulty, in a mixed economy, of predicting what changes will take place in private investment and foreign trade, it is all too easy for the Chancellor's advisers to get their sums wrong.

THE CHANCELLOR'S DIARY

The Budget itself is one item in a whole lot of regular annual activity by the Treasury. Apart from the key dates shown below, the Chancellor will also receive evidence and advice in the weeks before his Budget from all kinds of organisations and pressure groups, ranging from the TUC to the CBI, from firms of stockbrokers to Help The Aged.

NOVEMBER	results of official forecasting exercises become available to Chancellor
DECEMBER	Public spending estimates drawn up by government departments, co-ordinated and presented to Parliament
FEBRUARY	economic forecasts brought up to date and revised
MARCH 31	end of nation's *financial* year
DAY BEFORE BUDGET DAY	Cabinet informed of contents of Budget
*BUDGET DAY	Budget presented to Parliament
APRIL 5	end of nation's *tax* year
MAY 5	latest possible date for Government to renew its powers to collect taxes
LATER IN YEAR	supplementary Budgets as and when deemed necessary by Chancellor.

* Budget Day will be sometime in March, April or early May.

HOW UP TO DATE IS THE CHANCELLOR'S INFORMATION?

The Chancellor has to put together his Budget on the basis of information which is already out of date. Harold Macmillan said it was 'like trying to run the railways with last year's Bradshaw'.

Information on:	Out of date by:
Unemployment	
Vacancies	
Short-time working	
Bank lending	
Retail prices	2 months
Wholesale prices	
Exports	
Imports	
Wage rates	
Volume of retail trade	
Industrial production	
Average earnings	3 months
Balance of payments	
Investment	
Stockbuilding	
Consumers' expenditure	4 months
Total output	

The only really up-to-date information which the Chancellor will have to hand is the level of interest rates, the exchange value of the £ and the Financial Times Share Index.

MARGINS OF ERROR

■ Information

The information which the Chancellor has when he puts together his Budget is often inaccurate. Figures are often revised quite a lot in subsequent months and years as more new information becomes available.

For instance, in twelve of the fifteen years 1955-1969 the revisions made to the figure for consumer expenditure which he had at the time were greater than the change in tax revenue that he was trying to bring about with his Budget. In other words, in only three years out of the fifteen was the Chancellor's Budget intention greater than the margin of error in the key figure he was working from.

■ Forecasts

Margins of error are also a problem with forecasts. In the 1973 Budget, for instance, the forecast increase in imports between 1972 and 1973 was put at 7.2%. The actual increase which occurred was 10.8%, so that the increase was half as much again as was expected.

Prescription   It is on the basis of this imperfect information and advice that the Chancellor must formulate his Budget judgment about in what direction and how far he should try to steer the economy.

Failure to 'balance' the budget—keeping taxes in line with government spending—does not mean that the Chancellor has miscalculated. By manipulating taxes and government spending, he is trying to make good the failure of individual spending decisions to add up to the right total. He aims at eliminating the deflationary or inflationary gap. A Budget in which the Chancellor slashes taxes and increases State hand-outs is not generally a sign that the economy is prospering. It usually indicates that the Chancellor has diagnosed that we are heading for a recession and has therefore prescribed an injection of spending to avoid it. Similarly, budgeting for a surplus doesn't imply that the Chancellor has a lot to give away; what he is doing is effectively taking away a certain amount of purchasing power because we are trying to spend too much.

The Budget, then, isn't simply the method by which the Chancellor raises the necessary taxes to finance government expenditure. It is one of the ways in which governments try to manage the overall level of spending in the economy.

As well as altering their own income and spending, governments also try to manage the economy by influencing the private sector's decisions about output and expenditure. They can do so in a number of ways. Consumption can be stimulated or discouraged by changes in direct (income) or indirect (VAT, customs and excise) taxes and by relaxing or tightening up on HP deposit and repayment terms. Company investment plans can be influenced by changes in corporation tax, and by government grants and tax allowances for new plant and machinery. Devaluation, export credits and import controls can all be used to try to alter the balance between imports and exports.

But all these methods of treating the economic ill which the Chancellor thinks he has diagnosed are subject to two limitations. He doesn't know precisely by how much they will work, or when they will work. Investment can be encouraged by the government, but how far firms will respond depends on a host of factors beyond the government's direct control; the industrial horse can be led to water but it can't be made to drink. Similarly, it might be expected that personal spending will fall off when taxes are increased; but consumers may try to avoid this by reducing their savings. In the time that lapses between the introduction of measures and their beginning to bite, changes may have taken place in the economic situation which mean that they are no longer the appropriate treatment.

HITTING THE ECONOMIC TARGET

The Chancellor relies on getting four things right if his Budget is going to be effective.
■ The *direction* of the change he is trying to bring about.
If he boosts spending when it is already rising strongly, he might 'overheat' the economy. Similarly, if he cuts spending power when unemployment is rising, he might depress the economy too far.
■ The *amount* of change required.
If he raises spending too much, or cuts it too severely, he can overreach his target and bring about more inflation or recession.

■ The *timing* of the measures he selects. If he fails to take full account of how quickly a measure will begin to have its effect, the Chancellor is in danger of missing his target. The time-lags associated with Budget measures can stop the effects from appearing for several months.
■ The most *suitable* and *effective* measures. If the Chancellor selects measures which people can easily get round, or which have undesirable side-effects, he can simply create more problems for himself in the future.

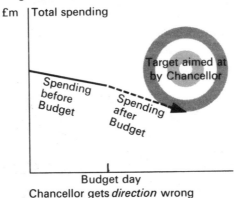

Chancellor gets *direction* wrong

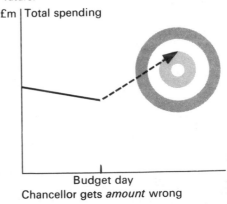

Chancellor gets *amount* wrong

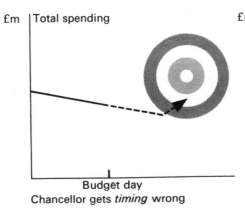

Chancellor gets *timing* wrong

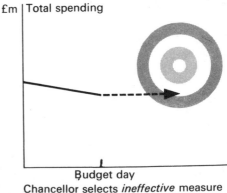

Chancellor selects *ineffective* measure

Most of these techniques are *Keynesian*—so-called because they are used to manage the level of total spending in the economy along the lines suggested by the breakthrough in economic thinking by John Maynard Keynes in the mid-thirties. Their systematic application during the postwar period has succeeded in avoiding the horrors of mass unemployment which plagued the interwar years. Where they have been found wanting though, is in the 'fine tuning' of the economy at which governments have aimed—delicately manipulating the level of spending to just the required amount.

Moreover, governments have not only been concerned with achieving high employment levels. They have worked towards a complex of economic objectives relating to jobs *and* prices *and* economic growth *and* the balance of payments. Two problems have arisen.

■ It has proved difficult to achieve all these objectives simultaneously: they have not always been compatible. Expansion of the economy has the short-run effect of stimulating imports—which the balance of payments may not be strong enough to stand. Alternatively, getting the international payments situation right may call for higher interest rates (to attract foreign funds) which deter domestic investment and threaten employment and growth.

■ It has become increasingly obvious that national economic objectives cannot be attained simply by manipulating spending. Cost inflation and economic growth, for example, need other measures—like prices and incomes policies or changes in the structure and efficiency of industry.

Keynesianism can help only to a degree and its limited success during the postwar period has led to a basic disagreement about the role of governments in the economy.

Treatment

On the Right, critics argue that by meddling with the economy, governments have made matters worse rather than better. For them, the answer is for governments to get out of the way and let the market get on with the job. In this, they have the theoretical backing of the Monetarists who claim that the use of a single regulator—controlling the money supply—would be a far more effective way of keeping the economy on the right course than the use of crude Keynesian techniques of demand management.

On the Left, the failures of Keynesianism are attributed to the fact that the behaviour of key sectors of the economy—like private investment and foreign trade—is impossible to predict because they are outside governments' direct control. On this view, what is needed is not less economic intervention, but intervention of a more direct and selective nature.

What has been presented here is necessarily a simplified version of the enormously complex game which the Chancellor has to play. For example, every government will have a view on what it thinks is the appropriate share-out between public and private spending. It is in the Budget that it stakes its claim on national resources by announcing not only tax rates but how much it will have to borrow to finance public spending.

THE GOVERNMENT'S BORROWING REQUIREMENT

The Budget surplus or deficit is only one element in the government's overall financial relationship with the rest of the economy. It is quite possible for the Budget to provide for a surplus of government revenue over government spending, whilst still leaving the government with the need to borrow large sums.

This was precisely the situation in the 1975-1976 financial year. The 1975 Budget planned for a surplus of current government revenue (mostly from taxes) over current spending of £1,200 million. But the government's capital expenditure (mostly long term investment) exceeded its capital receipts by £10,200 million. Its overall position was thus a shortfall of £9,000 million, which is its borrowing requirement.

Again, the preparation of the Budget is the time when the various government departments will put forward their opinions about how much ought to be spent within their own areas. Since these always add up to far more resources than the government has at its disposal, priorities have to be established. The Budget therefore represents a conflict between opposing departmental interests.

Finally, the Budget is an instrument for manipulating the social, as well as the economic, environment. In particular, it is concerned with bringing about a distribution of income and wealth which accords with the political philosophy of the party in power. But social and economic aims need not go hand in hand. It may be, for instance, that the economic objective of faster growth suggests that greater incentives should be offered (i.e. more inequality) while the government may be trying to promote greater equality as an end in itself. Part of the Chancellor's job is to achieve the proper balance. In this, there is no reason why economic aims should always be paramount. There are many situations, when the facts are spelled out, in which we would be prepared to accept an economic loss in order to achieve a social gain.

THE CHANCELLOR AND THE DOCTOR

There are many similarities between the Chancellor's budget and the doctor's approach to his patient:

Chancellor		Doctor
Review available statistics	**Both have to DIAGNOSE on the basis of**	Examine patient
Treasury advisers	**EXPERT KNOWLEDGE**	Medical training
Have we met the problem before?	**EXPERIENCE**	Is it a common complaint?
E.g., overheating due to rapid rise in consumer spending	**DIAGNOSIS**	Temperature caused by infection
Raise taxes, but which taxes? OR curb bank lending?	**Both then have to PRESCRIBE**	Medicine to reduce fever, and keep in an even temperature. But which medicine?
How much to raise taxes; how long to retain bank controls? (too much or too long can cause problems; too little may be ineffective)	**Both have to TREAT**	How much medicine? How often to be taken? (overdose can be dangerous, underdose ineffective)
How long before the measures bite?	**Both may have to worry about TIME-LAGS**	How quickly can the medicine work?
Is there tax evasion? Will people find ways round bank controls?	**Both have to keep an eye open for NON-CO-OPERATION and for**	Is the patient taking the medicine and staying indoors?
Is unemployment going to rise? Might investment suffer?	**POSSIBLE DANGEROUS SIDE-EFFECTS**	Might the medicine cause another kind of complaint?
Review statistics, and introduce a second Budget if necessary later in the year.	**And finally, both have to look at the problem again later**	Re-examine patient, and prescribe more or different kind of medicine if necessary.

YOUR PLACE IN THE ECONOMIC PUZZLE

YOU *DO* HAVE A SAY IN WHAT THE NATION PRODUCES

BUT YOUR SAY IS GETTING LESS AND LESS.

TV, radio and the press seem to devote more and more time and space to taking up consumers' grievances—often with seemingly effective results.

■ When did you last complain about something which you had bought and were not satisfied with?

■ Did you complain in the shop where you bought it, or write to the manufacturer?

■ Would your response be any different if you were dissatisfied with (a) private enterprise goods as opposed to (b) a nationalised industry service?

■ Do you often refuse to buy an alternative if your favourite brand is not available?

■ Have you recently begun to buy something new as a result of seeing TV commercials?

Your answers to these questions begin to indicate what kind of a consumer you are. And your behaviour as a consumer should help to influence the range of goods and services available and the prices charged for them. But does it?

■ Does the massive amount which firms spend on market research mean that they are really interested in discovering what your preferences are?

■ Or does the even greater amount spent on advertising mean that they are more interested in persuading you to buy what they want you to buy?

Would you be any better off as a consumer in an Eastern European centrally planned economy? These are the kind of questions to which this chapter turns as it tries to establish your place as a consumer in the economic puzzle.

The quart and the pint pot

So far we've been looking at how governments try (but don't always succeed) to provide a general economic framework of high employment, price stability and a satisfactory balance of payments—in which we can efficiently go about our business of producing and consuming and saving and investing.

But within that framework there remains the key question of what should be produced—and where, how and for whom? Who takes these decisions? Why do certain washing machines or cars or food-mixers suddenly disappear from the shops and showrooms to be replaced by new models? How is it that we produce Concordes and quadraphonic stereo systems while millions continue to live in substandard housing? It is sometimes said that we live in a consumer society. But do you and I really have any say, or are we at the mercy of big business and bureaucrats?

Before answering that question, we need to look at the fundamental economic problem which is common to all economic systems whether they be capitalist, socialist or communist. It is the problem of the quart and the pint pot.

The trouble is that we have nothing like enough resources to produce all the things which we would want to. Today, we consume goods and services on a scale which would have been quite unimaginable a couple of centuries ago. Yet we still ask for more. New wants are dreamed up even more quickly than our old ones are satisfied, but the means of satisfying them are limited and can't easily be increased. What, therefore, we are always trying to do is what is proverbially known to be impossible: to squeeze a quart out of a pint pot.

The quart

Consider the matter first in broad national terms. Most people would probably agree that having the items listed below would be a good thing, but roughly costed, the total bill might look something like this:

		Estimated cost (£000m.)
(i)	Adequate housing for all	50
(ii)	Improved National Health Service	50
(iii)	Proper provision for the aged	25
(iv)	Better education facilities	25
(v)	Modernisation of British industry	200
(vi)	A doubling of personal consumption	70
	TOTAL	420

The nature of the economic problem becomes clear when we set this £420,000 million quart of calls we would like to make on the economy against the pint pot of resources available to meet them:

The pint pot

- Natural resources like mineral deposits, a temperate climate or fertile soil.
- Human strengths, skills, knowledge and enterprise.
- Man-made capital—factories, machines, docks and roads.

Resources can be added to, for example, by industrial investment or the occasional bonus like the discovery of offshore oil; but at any one moment they are in very limited supply. In Britain they are enough at the present time to produce about £70,000 million of output a year.

THE ECONOMIST'S APPROACH

The economist approaches situations and problems with two key things in mind: *scarcity* and *cost*. It is clear that we can't have our 'quart' of wishes from the 'pint' of resources, so every bit of production in the economy means that something else is being foregone. This 'something else' is the *opportunity cost* of producing the item in question, and is the economist's way of measuring what sacrifice has been made.

- Within the government's education budget, the *opportunity cost* of building new universities may be measured in terms of not employing more teachers being able to raise the school-leaving age, or to reduce over-large classes in primary schools. If the government has one it cannot have the other.
- Within the public expenditure programme overall, the *opportunity cost* of doing anything in the education sector has to be measured in terms of what might otherwise have been done elsewhere, such as raising pensions, building a new motorway, or buying more military aircraft.
- And within total expenditure of all kinds, the *opportunity cost* of the government undertaking anything at all can be measured in terms of the loss of personal consumption (a new car or freezer, a holiday abroad, etc.),

which would be involved by the government having to take extra tax to pay for its own spending.

This opportunity cost, or economic cost, is not the same thing as an accountant's cost or a business cost. In some cases it can give a surprisingly different result. If for instance a coal mine or shipyard in Scotland was making a financial loss, then the owners would appear well-advised to close it down, and stop pouring good money after bad. But the principle of opportunity cost means that a wider question has to be answered before an economic judgement can reliably be made: 'Could the resources in the pit or shipyard be more productively used elsewhere, or for some other purpose?'

If the plant, machinery and workers cannot be transferred to other uses, either because
- they are specific to the particular form of production
- or because they are not easily moved to an alternative location
- or because there is already a high level of local or regional unemployment

then the economic cost of keeping the pit or shipyard open may be very small. This is because the alternative output which the workers could produce is nil—the opportunity cost is zero.

So the scarcity of resources means that we can't possibly have everything that we want. That's something that we are well used to as individuals. Agonising choices hound us from the cradle to the grave—sweets or comics, a film or an evening in the pub, a new washing machine or a summer holiday? With limited incomes, more of one means less of the other, and the same applies nationally. Slum clearance, better schools, industrial investment—all have to *compete* for the scarce resources which would have to be used to provide them.

At the extreme, there are two alternative ways in which these vital choices can be made. The pattern of output can be decided entirely through the market mechanism. Or it can be left to governments or planning bodies to determine what quantities of goods and services should be produced. In fact, no economy in the world relies exclusively on either method. All of them are mixed economies —with very different mixes. But whatever the system, where do *you* fit in?

You and the market

In the theory of the ideally working market mechanism, yours is the all-important role. It is consumers who rule the roost, and we do so by voting with our pockets. *We* signal to firms instructions about which goods they should produce and in what quantities. When we spend, it reflects the relative strength of *our* wants—and firms then pass on that message by getting hold of the amount of resources which *our* expenditure enables them to buy. In this way, resources are channelled into just those lines of production which *we* have dictated. The consumer is king.

The way in which we make our influence felt is by our reaction to the prices which firms charge.

■ For most goods, we signal our approval or disapproval to firms by buying more of their products at a lower price and less at a higher price.

■ The value that we set upon a product is also shown by how responsive we are to changes in price. In some cases, like foodstuffs, we may buy only very slightly less when the price goes up. An increase in the price of cinema seats, on the other hand, may evoke a much greater response as people opt to stay at home and watch television. The responsiveness of demand to price changes, the *elasticity* of demand, depends on the availability of close substitutes to which we can turn.

■ Changes in our tastes or incomes may mean that we are prepared to buy more or less of a product at the same price than we were before. A medical research report conclusively showing that watching colour television led to male impotence would doubtless cause a shift in demand which would mean that colour television manufacturers would sell fewer sets and therefore only be able to secure a smaller volume of resources. Our change of taste will bring about a switch of resources into making those things on which we spend more instead.

That is the theory. But how does it work in practice? There are those who argue that consumer sovereignty is a total myth.

They point to the fact that consumers are often too ignorant to make rational choices between competing products. How many of us are able to judge the real differences between soap powders, new cars or television sets?

This ignorance in turn makes us highly susceptible to advertising which so often seeks to persuade us to buy without offering any hard information about the product. In these circumstances, it is all too easy for the tail to begin to wag the dog. Big business, instead of responding to our demands, can itself create new wants which we would never have dreamed up for ourselves.

Then again, what the theory of the market suggests is that changes in consumer tastes causes a reshuffling of resources, but in practice these adjustments are often painfully slow or don't take place at all. Workers laid off in one industry may not easily be re-absorbed in other lines of production. The immobility of resources means that there are difficulties in shunting them between industries and areas.

The picture, then, which critics paint of the market system, is one in which consumer sovereignty has been usurped by producer power. It is firms which now manipulate and dictate to consumers, rather than consumers who call the tune.

Undoubtedly there has been a shift in recent decades in the balance of consumer and producer power, but consumers do still retain the ultimate sanction of saying 'no'—by not buying the goods which producers had hoped to force upon them. All is not quite lost. Collectively—and with the help of the media, consumer organisations like the publishers of *Which?* and protection from the government—we can become better informed, less easy prey to the blandishments of the advertisers, and more discriminating in judging products by their real quality and usefulness.

You and the State

The extreme alternative to a pure market economy (which doesn't exist anywhere) is a pure command economy (which also doesn't exist anywhere). A command economy is one in which decisions about production are made by a State planning body either on the basis of what it thinks consumers want or what it thinks they ought to have.

All economies have command elements—and only partly because of the failures of the market mechanism which we have just been looking at. It is also justified by the fact that, even to the extent that consumer sovereignty does prevail, some consumers are more sovereign than others. The unequal distibution of income means that the market is geared to catering for the wants of the rich rather than the needs of the poor. It is always being said that there is a housing shortage in this country. In fact, there is no such shortage of houses— for those who can afford to buy them. The trouble is that millions of people earn too little ever to register their needs by entering the housing market. If, therefore, we believe that everyone has the right to decent shelter, then either incomes have to be made more equal or we must introduce a command element into ensuring that homes are built for those who would be excluded if they were left to fend for themselves in the market.

But just suppose that we did all earn roughly the same, would you be prepared even then to say that areas like education, health and defence could safely be left for the market to provide—and that we should each of us be free to choose how much we spent on them? In the case of education and health, it might be that you would still argue: 'No, these are matters too important for the consumer to be completely sovereign. Parents ought to be made to ensure that their children have certain levels of schooling. People should not be allowed to choose to neglect the state of their health.' And with regard to defence—and the provision of police and fire services and the like—it is clearly impracticable for different individuals to be allowed to opt for or against them. Either we collectively agree that they should be provided—or we don't have them at all.

Three problems arise about the command element in an economy.

■ How far should it extend? It may be one thing to accept that the State should be responsible for education and quite another to allow the planners to dictate what range of toothpastes or dresses or kitchen gadgets should be made available.

■ How can we make sure that the command element is run efficiently? Ways have to be devised of ensuring that the absence of 'the discipline of the market' does not simply lead to waste.

■ How can the individual make his voice heard? This is the central issue which we have been discussing in this chapter and it arises about the consumer's relationship with bureaucrats as well as firms. How can the situation be avoided in which the authorities engaged in slum clearance can be unaware or uninterested in whether people *want* to be shifted into high-rise flats or new estates?

These are issues which we shall have to return to because so far *your* place in the economic puzzle has not yet been fully defined. But it does seem that under both market and command systems, the tendency has been for the consumer to be reduced to a pawn in the game, rather than the king. In the next two chapters we shall be looking at the two systems in more detail. And there will still remain to be discussed, in Chapter 13, the fact that your place in the puzzle is not just as consumer but also as worker. The two roles can conflict because what you want as a consumer may have implications which you find intolerable as a worker.

GOVERNMENTS TRY TO MAKE UP FOR THE DEFICIENCIES OF THE MARKET. BUT THAT CREATES PROBLEMS TOO.

MUNICIPAL OFFICES

DEMAND OR COMMAND?

What are the advantages of a market economy as compared to a command economy? The points below set out some of the disadvantages of each:

Market economy

■ Production may be distorted so that the rich get what they want and the poor are left out (e.g. luxury office blocks rather than old people's homes)

■ The market may operate to reinforce and widen these inequalities (e.g. concentration of personal ownership of shares into few hands)

■ Market forces may be restricted by monopoly elements with undue power over prices and production levels (such as dominant producers of building materials, or closed-shop industrial trade unions)

■ Resources may not be sufficiently mobile to allow market forces to operate (this can apply to land, labour and capital)

■ Consumers may have insufficient or incorrect information about goods and services (irresponsible advertising and artificial product differentiation are examples here)

■ At the international level, market forces can leave great power in the hands of the 'multinational' companies (e.g. they can choose which country to take their main profit in as a result of their internal pricing policies).

Command economy

■ Resources may be wasted by not being used where their efficiency is highest (e.g. the deliberate encouragement of 'prestige' industries, such as aerospace, which have very high opportunity costs).

■ Neither prices nor production levels may be responsive to changes in consumer demand (shortages and long waiting lists are symptoms of this).

■ The planners' decisions may not closely reflect people's genuine preferences or their social priorities (e.g. improvements in public transport may be held back in favour of subsidies to agriculture).

■ Production can become geared to *quantity*, with insufficient attention to quality or suitability (when Yugoslavia was a centrally planned economy after the war, the adoption of production targets for glasses led to over-production of glasses which were too small to contain a bottle of beer).

■ Problems arising from the lack of incentives can emerge, as producers decide it is not worth making extra effort in the absence of extra profits (again quality can suffer and wastages occur).

■ The power of the planners and of the key industries can lead to bureaucracy, privilege and corruption.

■ The overriding of market forces in favour of certain kinds of production can lead to imbalance and unfairness in the context of international trade.

APPENDIX:

THE MARKET MECHANISM

The chapter has mentioned three principles of consumer demand. This Appendix shows in more detail how the economist looks at demand and how this can be illustrated graphically.

First principle

■ *The higher the price of the good, the less is likely to be the demand for it.*

The word 'demand' can mean the demand of an individual, demand at a shop, demand for a firm's product, the total demand of all consumers in the economy. To be meaningful we must always refer to demand within a particular period (a day, week, month or year).

How to construct a demand schedule.

Consider a shop selling pocket calculators. A couple of years ago they were priced at £50 each, and the shop only sold one a week on average. Today they are priced at only £10 each, and the shop sells ten a week. This illustrates the principle that the lower the price, the higher the demand. This principle rests firmly upon the notion of opportunity cost referred to in the chapter. That is to say, the lower the price of one good, the less other goods that have to be sacrificed in order to buy the first good.

To return to our pocket calculators, the shop's record of demand at different price levels may well look like this:

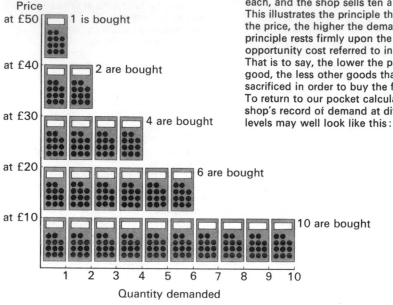

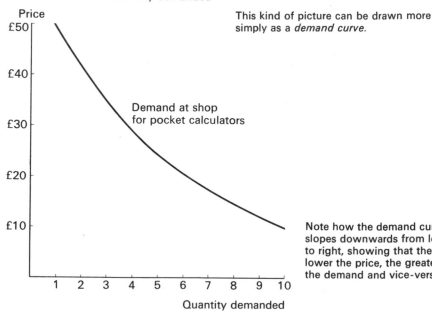

This kind of picture can be drawn more simply as a *demand curve*.

Note how the demand curve slopes downwards from left to right, showing that the lower the price, the greater the demand and vice-versa.

CONSUMER DEMAND

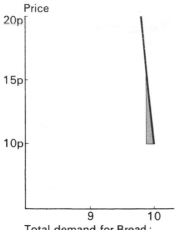

Total demand for Bread:
million loaves per day

Demand for bread is *inelastic*. A larger rise
in price from 10p to 15p, or about 50%)
brings about a small change in demand
(from 10 million to 9.8 million or 2%).

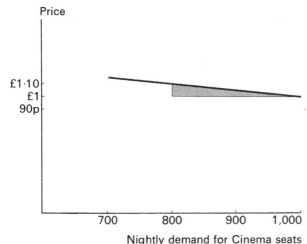

Nightly demand for Cinema seats

Demand for cinema seats is *elastic*. A small
price rise (from £1.00 to £1.10, or 10%)
causes a large drop in demand (from 1,000
to 800 or 20%).

Second principle:
■ *The slope of the demand curve shows
the responsiveness of demand to a change
in price of the good.*
If there are no close substitutes or alternatives for a particular good, and If there are
practical limits to how much of it an
individual or family can usefully do with
over a period of time, then consumer
demand is unlikely to respond very much to
a change in price of the good.
A good example of this would be bread.
There are no obvious substitutes in the
British diet, so people have to continue to
buy the same amount despite price rises. At
the same time, they are hardly likely to buy
ten times the amount of bread they
normally do if its price were to become
much lower.
The demand curve for bread therefore
slopes downward sharply, showing that
quite large changes in price have to occur
before the demand for it alters much.
It is only if the price of bread were to
become very high that people would consider less obvious alternatives such as pasta
or rice. The economist calls the demand for
such goods *inelastic*: the percentage
change in demand is less than the
percentage change in price.
By contrast, the demand for a good which
has close competitive substitutes will be
very sensitive and responsive to changes in
price. This is particularly true for luxury
goods which people would ideally like more
of but which they can do without if necessary. The example taken here is cinema
seats, for there are lots of alternative forms
of entertainment available, and films are not
an essential part of people's staple diet.
With such goods the demand curve will
be fairly flat and horizontal, showing that
a small price change can cause a big
change in demand. The economist calls the
demand for such goods *elastic*: the %
change in demand is greater than the
% change in price.

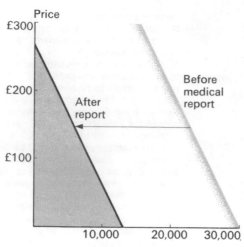

Price

A shift to the left of the demand curve (caused by a change in taste) means that demand is now less at any given price. Whereas before 20,000 sets were demanded at £200; after, the demand at that price is only 3,000.

Third principle

■ *A change in either the taste or the income of consumers causes a* shift *of their demand curve.*

It is essential to distinguish between the effect of a change in price of the good, which you can observe by looking along the demand curve, and a change in the taste or income of consumers, which means that you have to draw a new curve—the original curve shifts.

This chapter referred to the possible effect of a medical report on the demand for colour TVs. The effect would be a shift to the left of the curve.

To illustrate a shift to the right of a demand curve, think what would happen to the demand for wine if consumer incomes increase. It is just the sort of thing that people will buy more of (economists call this *income-elastic*), and so the curve shifts to the right.

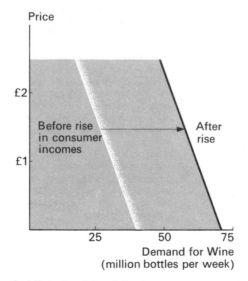

Price

A shift to the right of the demand curve (caused by a rise in income) means that demand is now more at any given price, whereas before less than 25 million bottles were demanded at £2, the demand after that price is over 50 million bottles.

YOU'VE ALL HEARD OF DEMAND AND SUPPLY—UNDERSTANDING THEM IS A CRUCIAL PART OF ECONOMICS.

When you hear of people paying ten times the face value of cup final tickets to the touts outside Wembley Stadium do you:
■ feel sorry for people being exploited in this way, and feel that touting should be banned? or
■ say that if people are daft enough to pay that kind of money, then good luck to the touts?
Whichever way you feel, you are looking at a situation of supply and demand. The economist's approach to this kind of situation can be used to explain all sorts of problems that even the most ardent football fan would agree were more important and wide-ranging than the example above.

■ Why have food prices increased so much over the past few years?
■ Why are house prices higher in the South than the North?
■ How was it that Britain got richer as a nation during the world depression of the 1930s?
These are some of the questions that can be answered by reference to the workings of the market mechanism and in particular supply and demand. This chapter takes a more detached look at these key economic ideas and anyone who finds the approach too technical for them should move on to Chapter 11.

Rapid inflation blurs the fact that although nearly everything we buy is becoming more expensive, prices haven't all risen at the same rate. Inflation of 20% means that prices on average have gone up by that amount. For some things, the increase has been far greater. For others, it has been markedly less. So what determines the value of one product in terms of another, i.e. the changes in their *relative* prices?

How prices are fixed

Everything has its price—and so, it is said, has everybody. That price is the result of the opposing forces of demand and supply. The price which people are prepared to pay for something reflects the strength of their desire for it. And in the same way that a demand curve can be built up which shows the amounts that consumers would be willing to buy at different prices, so also producers' plans can be illustrated in the form of a *supply* curve.

Think, for example, about a manufacturer of colour televisions with a factory which can comfortably turn out a thousand sets a week. In the long run, he could replace that factory with a smaller one or a larger one. But even in the short run, he will have a certain amount of flexibility about the amount that he produces. In the short run, how many he decides to produce depends on the price which he can get for them.

Turning out a thousand sets a week to be sold at £200 each makes him a satisfactory profit. He could make 1,200 sets—but only by introducing overtime and week-end working. And he will therefore only do so if he gets a price, say £250, high enough to cover his increased costs. Even more output may be squeezed out if the firm goes over to shift work—perhaps 2,000 sets a week.

But that means a further jump in the firm's unit costs—because half the work-force is now on night rates, because the firm is having to bid workers away from other jobs in the area, and because more has to be spent on maintenance if the machinery is to be kept running. The firm will only be prepared to produce those 2,000 sets if the price is much higher—say £300.

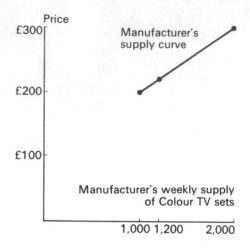

HOW TO READ DEMAND AND SUPPLY CURVES AND SEE WHAT FIXES PRICES

(i) **Find where the two curves cross.**
(ii) **Look straight** *down* **and note the** number of sets supplied and demanded.
(iii) **Return to where the two curves cross.** Look straight *across* to see the price which results.

It is only at a price of £200 that what producers plan to supply and what consumers plan to buy are equal.

Take any price other than £200. Draw a line across. Where it cuts the demand and supply curves, draw lines downwards and read off how many TV sets would be demanded and supplied. You will find that at a price above £200, supply will exceed demand. At a price below £200, demand for TV sets will be greater than the number supplied.

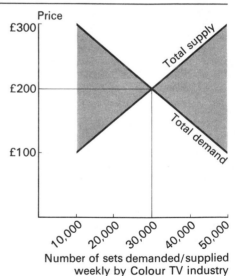

The interests of consumers and producers therefore collide. What consumers are after are low prices; the demand curve shows that as prices rise, they buy less. Producers, on the other hand, are out to charge as much as they can; the higher the price they can get, the more they are willing to market. Consumers and producers have largely incompatible plans about what they would do at different prices. The actual price which results is a compromise between the two. It is a price at which what consumers are prepared to buy just matches what producers are willing to offer for sale. The price of something reflects not only the strength of consumer demand for it but also the relative scarcity of the resources which go into making it.

It is through this mechanism of prices that you, at least ideally, are able to have some say in the way in which resources are used. If you and others are convinced that Guinness makes for long life, then the demand curve for Guinness will shift to the right—showing that consumers are keen to buy more Guinness even at a higher price. Therefore, the higher price which the brewers now get enables them to buy the larger amounts of materials and labour which they need to quench their customers' increased thirst.

Exactly the same sort of analysis can be used to explain some of the major changes in relative prices which have actually been taking place in recent

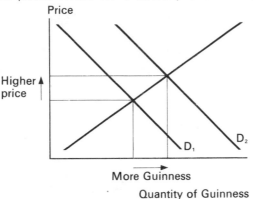

PRICE MOVEMENTS
IN 1974

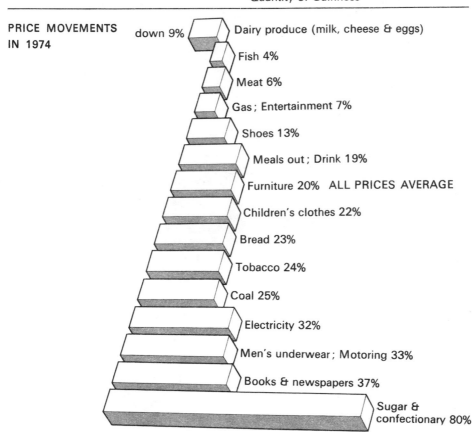

down 9% Dairy produce (milk, cheese & eggs)

Fish 4%

Meat 6%

Gas; Entertainment 7%

Shoes 13%

Meals out; Drink 19%

Furniture 20% ALL PRICES AVERAGE

Children's clothes 22%

Bread 23%

Tobacco 24%

Coal 25%

Electricity 32%

Men's underwear; Motoring 33%

Books & newspapers 37%

Sugar & confectionary 80%

years. Undoubtedly, the one which has affected people most has been the spectacular explosion which has taken place in food prices.

Why food prices have exploded

Neither the demand nor the supply of food is very sensitive to price changes—they are both said to be *inelastic*. Food is something which we have to buy more or less the same amount of regardless of price, and natural factors make it difficult for producers to increase output when prices rise or reduce it when prices fall. This unresponsiveness to price changes means that both the demand and the supply curves for food are likely to be rather steeply inclined.

The main upsurge in food prices took place in 1973-4 and was the result of *shifts* in both the demand and supply curves. Most food output is consumed in the countries which produce it, leaving only relatively small surpluses available for world trade. Every year, the calls on these surpluses are increased by the growth of world population. But on top of that in 1973-4, there were failures in the USSR and Chinese harvests which led to both of these countries increasing their imports of food. In other words, the demand curve for food shifted to the right—showing, that at any given price, consumers were willing to buy more food than before. Simultaneously, however, the supply curve was shifting to the left; farmers were prepared to supply less at any given price than previously. This was mainly due to the increased cost of fertilisers and a reduction in the scale of the United States farm support programme.

The combination of reduced supply and increased demand was enough to send food prices in the western world soaring.

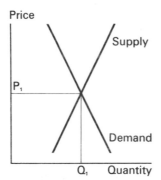

Both supply and demand of food are *inelastic*. Price before developments was P_1 and the amount produced and demanded was Q_1.

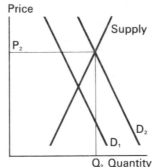

Demand curve for food shifts to right due to population increase and harvest failures. New price becomes P_2, and new amount Q_2.

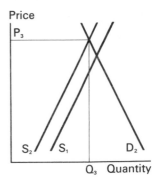

At the same time the supply curve shifted to left as farmers became tougher. After all these developments price is now P_3 and amount produced and demanded is Q_3.

Why houses are dearer in the south

Generalising broadly, there are three main reasons why buying a house in the south is a more costly business than setting up home in the north.

■ Incomes in the north tend to be lower than those in the south—which affects the demand for housing.

■ The net emigration from the north, particularly of younger people, both reduces the demand for houses and leaves a greater supply available for sale.

■ Building land is more abundant in the north than in the congested south.

Together, these factors mean that the supply and demand conditions for houses, and therefore their prices, are very different.

Why Old Masters and pop stars command such high prices

What do a Rembrandt and Tom Jones have in common? Well, firstly they are both in great demand. And secondly, supply of them is completely limited.

The supply curve for each of them is therefore vertical. That is, regardless of the price paid for them, the supply of that particular picture and that particular pop star cannot be increased.

Their price is therefore entirely determined by demand—which, for very different reasons, happens to be extremely high in both cases.

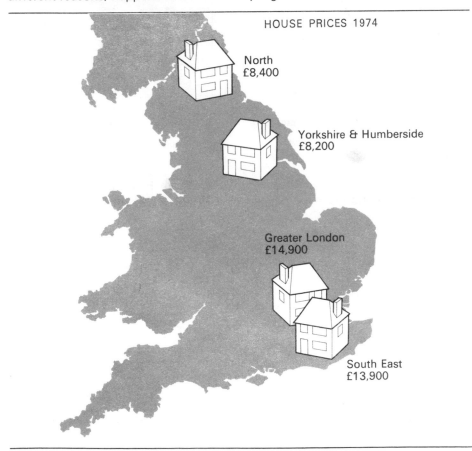

HOUSE PRICES 1974

North
£8,400

Yorkshire & Humberside
£8,200

Greater London
£14,900

South East
£13,900

Why Britain got richer during a world slump

One final example will show how simple supply and demand analysis can be used to throw some light on quite complex events. The nineteen-thirties slump was a somewhat paradoxical episode for Britain. It was a period of intense depression, mass unemployment and general economic distress. And yet the fact is that during these years, the average real income in Britain actually rose. As a nation, we became better off.

The explanation lies in Britain's position as a major importer of primary goods (food and raw materials) and exporter of manufactured goods. As we have already suggested, the demand and supply of primary goods are both likely to be unresponsive to changes in prices. The demand for manufactured products, on the other hand, since many of them are non-essentials, *is* sensitive to price changes. Their supply, too, can be much more easily adjusted. In the short run, more output can generally be produced from existing factories when prices rise—and it can also easily be reduced by laying off labour. And in the long run, building more factories poses fewer problems than increasing the amount of land under cultivation.

The demand and supply curves for manufactured goods are therefore much flatter than those for primary products.

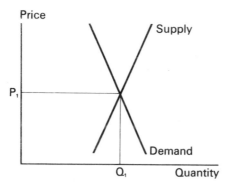

Demand and supply of primary goods are both *inelastic*.

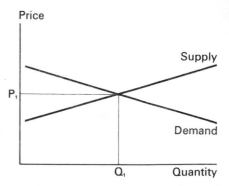

Demand and supply of manufactured goods are both *elastic*.

Now consider the impact of a world depression. How does this alter the picture? With world incomes reduced as a result, the demand curves shift to the left.

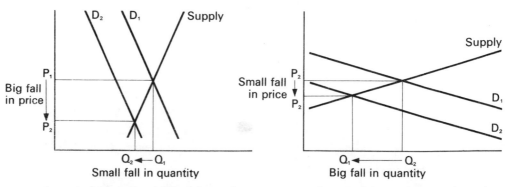

Impact of depression (shift of demand curve to left) on price of primary goods greater than effect on output.

Impact of depression on prices of manufactured goods less than on output.

UNEMPLOYMENT

What is interesting is the marked difference in the effects which this has on the price and output of the two types of goods. Because the supply curve is much steeper (i.e. supply could not be contracted very much in response to the fall in demand), the price of primary products fell dramatically faster than that of manufactured goods. That is why Britain got richer in the nineteen-thirties. The prices of our imports fell far more than the prices of our exports so that we were able to buy a larger volume of imports for any given volume of exports. (This is known as a favourable movement in the 'terms of trade'.)

Note also the different impact of reduced demand on output in the primary producing and manufacturing countries. It fell only slightly in the case of the primary producers (and, indeed, it was just this failure of production to respond to reduced demand which threw the burden of adjustment on to price). The output of manufactured goods, in contrast, was drastically cut down. That, of course, meant unemployment. Thus although Britain as a nation got richer during the slump because of cheaper imports, the benefits went only to those lucky enough to hold on to their jobs.

The purpose of this chapter has been to show the market at work, and to give the non-economist some impression of how economists set about analysing market situations. But, as we were arguing in the last chapter, the market in practice often works very imperfectly and requires State intervention if a socially acceptable outcome is to be achieved. It is to the nature of the State's role that we turn in Chapter 11.

FINAL DEMAND

Returning to the question of cup final tickets mentioned, can you now answer the following questions with reference to supply and demand:

■ How can more be charged for the cup final than any other match?

■ How is it that touts can get ten times the price for their tickets on the day?

Consider the following:

■ The *supply* of tickets is very limited: it is *inelastic*. Not only are there only 100,000 in total, but they are carefully rationed out.

■ The cup final is unique: there is no close substitute, so *demand* is also *inelastic*.

■ Demand is very high in relation to supply, both among the finalist clubs' supporters and among football fans in general.

■ On the day of the final, demand is even higher in relation to supply, which is now limited to the touts' tickets.

It is only if demand for the touts' tickets were to become *elastic* at the high prices they were charging that they would get their fingers burnt, and be left with a very perishable product on their hands.

What do the following have in common?
■ policeman, teacher, dustman, nurse, fireman?
■ pensioner, unemployed or redundant worker?
■ hospital, school, library, council house?

■ In the first group, all are employees of the State.
■ In the second group, all receive an income from the State.
■ In the third group, all are built by the State.

The State's role in the modern economy is very wide-ranging; do you think it is too great, and that certain activities would be better left to the private sector?
Or, if you are happy with the degree of State influence, are you equally happy with the levels at which decisions are taken; are our local councils losing their powers to Whitehall?
These are some of the questions which this chapter looks at in an effort to identify what should be the State's role and the problems which the financing of this role brings about.

Most people resent the way in which the taxman confiscates part of their hard-earned incomes. Behind much of that resentment lurks the suspicion that we are being bled just to subsidise government extravagance and waste. And yet we also complain when the axe falls on services like education or when bus subsidies are withdrawn or school meal charges are increased—all of which are ways of holding taxes down.

It's difficult always to keep in mind the connexion between the taxes which we pay and the range of public services which are available as a result—services which are just as much a part of our standard of living as private consumption of cars and clothing and all the other things on which we spend what's left of our income after the taxman has had his bite.

We are right to demand that the authorities should be economical when it comes to spending tax revenue. But it is important to distinguish between:
■ Economies which ensure that public services are run in the most efficient way—so that we get the best value for our money.
■ Economies which involve making cuts in the range and quality of the services which are provided.

We all want the first sort of economy. We may or may not want the second. That is one of the main questions for this chapter—whether the State should provide still more services or if it is already taking on too much. We shall also look into who decides about public spending and how it is all financed. But first, why do governments provide services at all? Why don't they just leave us to spend our incomes entirely as we choose to?

Why have public services at all?

During the postwar period, the proportion of total national spending undertaken by government authorities has gradually increased up to its present level of about 50%. This has been due more to the increase in State 'transfer payments' from one section of the community to another (such as providing old age pensions out of social security contributions) than to an increase in the State's direct spending on its own behalf.

Of the resources becoming available to Britain in 1973, about one-fifth went on investment and the rest on consumption. Of the amount spent on investment:
■ 15% was spent by the nationalised industries.
■ another 25% was spent by other public bodies, including central and local government, on schools, hospitals, houses, roads, etc.

Of the amount spent on consumption:
■ a quarter was directly consumed by the public sector on health, education, defence and police, etc.
■ another fifth was financed by benefits and subsidies provided by the government.

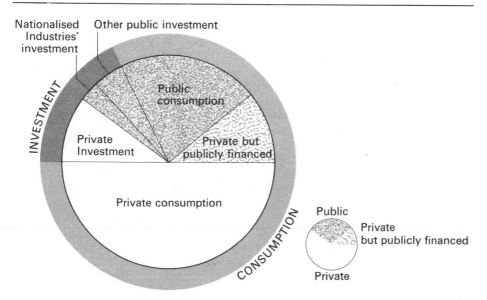

HOW THE MONEY IS SPENT

The main items of public expenditure on goods and services are (1974-1975 figures):
Defence 18%
Health and personal social services 18%
Education 17%
Nationalised industries 10%
Housing 8%
Other environmental 7%
Roads and transport 6%
Law and order 5%

The main forms of transfer payments by the State are:
Social security 36%
Commerce and industry 17%
Housing 11%
Education 5%

What is the justification for the public sector commandeering such a sizeable slice of the national cake? The basic rationale has already been spelled out in Chapter 9. It depends on whether the market mechanism can be relied upon to provide these services fairly and on the required scale. Grounds for doubt vary with different types of services.
■ Services like defence or policing from which it is simply not practicable to

allow individuals to opt out, and which therefore have to be provided on an all-or-nothing basis.

■ Services which the market *could* supply but which might cause unfairness because of the unequal distribution of income, e.g. recreation grounds which would be used mostly by those least able to pay for them.

■ Services on which we think that individuals should *not* be free to decide how much they spend—like education and health.

■ Services for which the demand is created by private affluence but where costs are difficult to recoup via the market, e.g. roads and traffic lights.

There are some economists who claim that these arguments for the public provision of services have been greatly overplayed. It has led to government spending on a wastefully extensive scale—and a quite unnecessary restriction of individual free choice. Under our present system, State benefits like secondary education or health care are handed out on a universal basis regardless of individual need. Wouldn't it be more sensible to concentrate on helping those who need it and to leave the better-off to fend for themselves out of their own incomes? Benefits granted on a selective basis could massively reduce the present level of State spending. Suggestions have been put forward for replacing automatic State provision by the market mechanism, not only with regard to education and health, but also in areas like refuse collection, sewage disposal and road use. The object is to reintroduce prices as an indication of how strongly people *want* particular services, and to shift the burden of providing them from the taxpayer to the consumer. Only those consumers below stipulated income levels should be subsidised by government.

Whether governments should provide more public services or less is a question which can't be answered by economics alone. How great public sector provision should be is also a matter of political ideology. It involves a value judgment about the nature of the society in which we want to live. Should the individual's right to choose for himself how to spend his income be all important—at the cost of subjecting people to what some would regard as the indignity of means-testing and the risk that there will be those who freely choose to neglect their own health or their children's education? Does the co-existence of public and private provision of services carry the danger that those who would have been the most vocal in demanding improvement in the public sector will probably have opted for private provision? Is collective consumption desirable in itself—in cultivating a more egalitarian environment?

And once the major political issue about the size of public sector provision of services is resolved, three questions still remain to be answered:

■ Who decides which services should be provided, and of what quality?

■ Who then does the actual spending?

■ Who foots the bill?

Deciding

Deciding which services should be supplied and on what scale is almost entirely the responsibility of central government—the Ministers at Whitehall. How much should be spent, and in what ways, on social security, housing, education and health are all matters laid down from above. Local authorities in the town halls have relatively little discretionary power.

Spending

When it comes to spending, however, the local authorities become an extremely important part of the government operation. Nearly 30% of total government expenditure is by local councils. But only a relatively small part of this goes in paying for services decided upon by the councils themselves. The rest takes the form of local authorities acting as agents for central government departments in implementing *their* policies.

WHO DOES WHAT?

■ Since the war the central government has withdrawn many key areas away from the local councils, including:
gas, electricity, hospitals, community health and family planning, water, and certain elements of education and housing.

■ It has also placed greater obligations on local councils to standardise practice and meet stipulated levels of service—like spending money on priority areas of severe social deprivation, provision (or rather non-provision!) of school milk, comprehensive education and rent levels.

■ Against this the central government has moved away from specific grants which have to be spent on a stipulated project towards block grants which leave more freedom of emphasis to the local authority.

■ There has also been a greater degree of flexibility in the loan sanctions given as permission for local authority borrowing.

■ But despite these apparent moves towards greater local decision-making powers, the central government retains the ultimate right to lay down spending guidelines and to vary the grants it makes available to support the income from local rates if it feels councils are stepping too far out of line.

■ Finally, the government at Westminster is unlikely to loosen its grip on local authority spending as long as it retains the ultimate responsibility for economic policy. The wish to encourage investment and trying to control inflation mean that central government has to have a finger in the local pie.

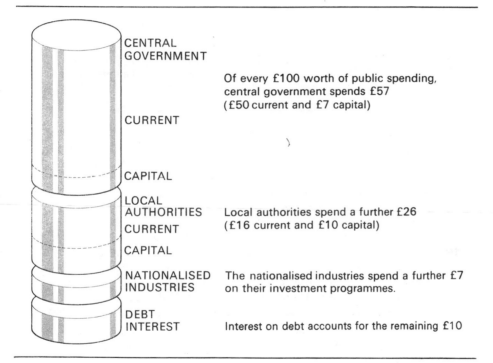

CENTRAL GOVERNMENT

CURRENT

Of every £100 worth of public spending, central government spends £57
(£50 current and £7 capital)

CAPITAL

LOCAL AUTHORITIES

CURRENT

Local authorities spend a further £26
(£16 current and £10 capital)

CAPITAL

NATIONALISED INDUSTRIES

The nationalised industries spend a further £7 on their investment programmes.

DEBT INTEREST

Interest on debt accounts for the remaining £10

Financing for the running of State services comes from three sources—central government tax revenue, national insurance contributions and local authority rates.

As well as the money for their day-to-day working, State services also require capital expenditure—for the building of hospitals, schools, roads, etc. This is largely financed by public borrowing, and, once again, the local authorities have an important role to play in raising loans.

This sharing between central and local government of responsibility for running and paying for public services can lead to a lot of acrimony between Whitehall and the town halls as each tries to divert public attention to the shortcomings of the other.

Financing

Whitehall versus the town hall

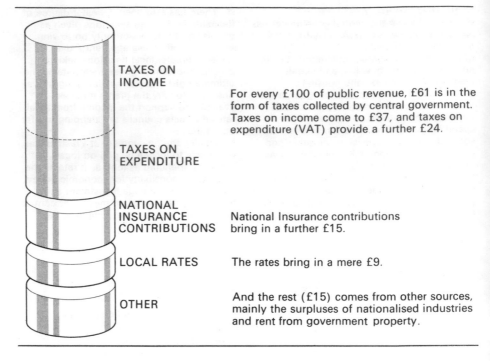

TAXES ON INCOME

For every £100 of public revenue, £61 is in the form of taxes collected by central government. Taxes on income come to £37, and taxes on expenditure (VAT) provide a further £24.

TAXES ON EXPENDITURE

NATIONAL INSURANCE CONTRIBUTIONS

National Insurance contributions bring in a further £15.

LOCAL RATES

The rates bring in a mere £9.

OTHER

And the rest (£15) comes from other sources, mainly the surpluses of nationalised industries and rent from government property.

What happens is this. As we have already seen, decisions about which services should be provided are largely taken at the centre but many of them are then administered by the local authorities. Their cost has soared in recent years, partly because of inflation and partly because central government has extended the range of services or demanded an improvement in their quality. How then does the local authority set about meeting these cost increases?

First of all, it is entitled to a *rate support grant* from the central government. This in 1975-1976 will account for no less than two-thirds of its total spending. But the basis on which the support grant is calculated still leaves the local authority with the unpopular task of having to increase its income from rates.

The problem with rates is that they don't rise automatically with inflation in a way which is meaningful to those who pay them. With income tax, we all pay more year by year—but we do see that it is because our incomes are also rising

---

THE RATE SUPPORT GRANT
At the beginning of each year local authorities estimate their expected spending on everything except housing (which the government deals with separately by subsidies). The government then undertakes to pay a block grant which has three elements:
■ *The needs element* reflects the services a local authority provides, and is based upon the number of local inhabitants receiving the various services. It is thus largely school-children and old people who are reflected in the size of the needs element.
■ *The resources element* is paid to local authorities with a relatively low rateable

value per head, which in practice means those with sub-standard resources.
■ *The domestic element* is a direct subsidy to ratepayers expressed as so many pence in the pound. Its impact can vary considerably from one local authority to another.

In 1975-1976:
■ The needs element came to £2,700 million;
■ The resources element was about £1,300 m.;
■ The domestic element knocked 18½p off the rate poundage in England and 36p in Wales. Without it, rates would be 25% higher.

LOCAL AUTHORITY BORROWING

Most of the finance for local authorities' capital expenditure is raised by loans, with the result that 20% of their total current spending goes on repaying them. However the local authorities' contribution to the government's overall borrowing requirement has fallen substantially in recent years:

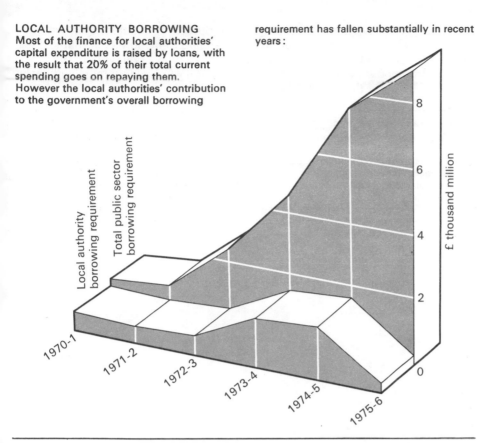

Local authority borrowing requirement

Total public sector borrowing requirement

£ thousand million

1970-1
1971-2
1972-3
1973-4
1974-5
1975-6

THEY'RE UP EVERY YEAR. IT'S ABSOLUTELY CRIPPLING.

RATE DEMAND

as a result of inflation. But rates are a tax on property. And although the value of the property also generally increases with inflation, we don't immediately connect that fact with the rate increases payable on it.

Local government is therefore often in an unenviable position. For political reasons, Whitehall may be issuing instructions that rises in local rates must be kept within acceptable limits. And yet, at the same time, the need to raise rates stems mainly from the central government asking the local authorities to be responsible for an ever-mounting range of services.

So when we vent our rage on the local council for increasing rates year by year, we are sometimes missing the real target. But would it be better therefore if more services were transferred onto a national basis and financed out of general taxation? One problem with that is that it would be even more difficult to get redress for our complaints from a remote Whitehall official than it is from our local councillor. Or should rates be replaced by an alternative source of local finance—more geared to inflation and more obviously related to ability to pay? The Layfield Commission is currently looking at such alternatives—like lotteries, and local income or sales tax.

However the system may be re-jigged, we will still have to pay in one way or another. Is the problem, then, that we have finally reached the limit of our tax patience? It is certainly a popularly held view that the British are taxed much more heavily than others. But the facts don't bear this out.

And so in the end we come back to the basic importance of seeing the connexion between the taxes which we pay and the benefits which we enjoy

All income taxes, taxes on expenditure and social security contributions as a % of total national output, 1972:

Denmark	50.9
Austria	43.5
France	42.0
Germany	41.9
Belgium	39.3
U.K.	38.3
Italy	33.9
USA	33.7
Japan	21.4

as a result. When we demand relief from the burden of taxation, then we must accept the cut in the social element in the standard of living which that implies. It used to be said of love and marriage that you can't have one without the other. That may no longer be true. But it still holds good of providing more and better public services and the need to pay for them.

A POOR RATE OF PROGRESS?
Total taxes as % of National Output
Rates are clearly not a 'buoyant' source of income compared with other taxes. But the situation facing local authorities has been even more alarming as far as rates are concerned since 1970:

■ because inflation has accelerated, raising revenue from income taxes but not anywhere near so much from rates.

■ because inflation has increased the cost of providing local authority services in particular, mainly due to their high wage and salary component.

■ because the combined result is that the gap between local authority spending requirements and their revenue from their only independent form of income has widened.

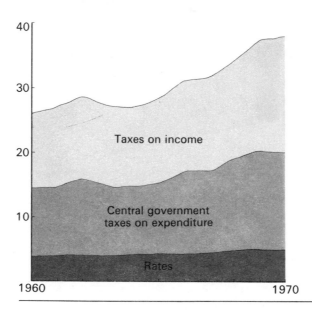

THE NATIONALISATION BOGEY

12

> NATIONALISED INDUSTRIES ARE DIFFERENT FROM PRIVATE ENTERPRISE AND SHOULD NOT THEREFORE BE JUDGED BY PROFITABILITY ALONE.

The British Rail modern symbol is no doubt supposed to represent the up-line and the down-line, but it would be equally apt as a reminder that nationalised industries have two sets of reasoning behind them which tend to pull in opposite directions. These two directions are often to be found in our own attitudes to nationalised industries:
■ are nationalised industries inefficient compared with private enterprise?
■ should they be made to run more on lines of profit?

■ or should they operate first and foremost 'in the national interest', providing our key services as cheaply as possible?
These are very difficult questions to which clear and lasting answers have proved very elusive. Not only is the economics of nationalised industries a complex area, but also they have tended to become political footballs or hostages of the political parties. This chapter aims to set out and begin to answer some of the questions concerning our nationalised industries.

A lot of people tend to get rather worked up when they talk about nationalisation. It's a subject on which most of us hold strong views. For some, they're just a rather unfunny music hall joke—inefficient, unreliable, bureaucratic money-losers lacking the dynamism of private enterprise. But for others, nationalisation represents a vital State control over the commanding heights of the economy, a step towards a more humanely socialist society not wholly dominated by private profit.

Arguments about nationalisation usually generate more heat than light. They are mostly about how much money the nationalised industries lose, how badly they are run, the exorbitant prices they charge because of their monopolistic positions, and the way in which their workers are always holding government and nation to ransom. Just how true are these allegations which are so frequently levelled at public enterprises?

> NATIONALISATION? IT'S MONEY DOWN THE DRAIN.

■ Certainly some of them do make losses and whether those are ever justified is a matter we shall come to shortly, but nationalised industries don't all make losses every year. Some have generally earned surpluses, others have had a mixed record—and only the railways have consistently lost money. Moreover, contrasting the losses of public enterprise with the profits of private enterprise is misleading because the comparison is not on a like-with-like basis. Most of a private company's capital is held by its shareholders who get dividends related to the profits earned. But nationalised industries don't generally have any share capital. Instead they are financed by loans on which they have to pay fixed interest. So a private firm which earns receipts more than its running costs is able to announce a profit which can be distributed as dividends. But when a public enterprise similarly makes a 'working profit', that may not be enough to meet its interest charges—in which case, instead of just paying a lower dividend as the private firm would, it is declared to be making a loss.

SURPLUSES *Before interest charges* £m.							SURPLUSES *After interest charges* £m.					
	69/70	70/71	71/72	72/73	73/74	74/75	69/70	70/71	71/72	72/73	73/74	74/75
British Rail	52	30	25	25	6	—86	15	10	—15	—26	—51	—158
Coal	9	36	—118	—39	—112	34	—26	1	—157	—83	—145	—2
British Steel Corporation	26*	49	—7	45	105	149	10*	15	—45	9	56	89
Post Office	147	152	121	123	96	—6	36	21	36	—64	—128	—307
Electricity Council	306	205	259	299	163	128	65	—56	—23	2	—166	—258
Gas Council	102	108	140	151	106	106	14	2	15	6	—50	—57
Total	642*	580	420	602	364	325	114*	—7	—189	—156	—484	—693

* British Steel Corporation figures are for six months only.

NATIONALISATION? IT'S ANOTHER WORD FOR SLOPPY INEFFICIENCY.

In 1968/69 the National Coal Bord had a surplus, of £29 million on the sales of £855 m and its assets of £722 million.
In the same year the Ford Motor Company had profits, before interest, of £43 million on its sales of £538 million and assets of £383 million.

EFFICIENCY
Increase in output per man-hour

	1948-58	1958-68
Nationalised industries	16%	68%
Private manufacturing industry	68%	44%

After interest charges of £38 million, the Coal Board's surplus became a deficit of £9 million.
After interest charges of £5 million and dividends paid on its shares of £12m, Ford could still retain £26 million profit.

■ Between 1958 and 1968 only one manufacturing industry (chemicals) had productivity increases more than in the nationalised industry sector.
■ In only one nationalised undertaking (buses) did productivity increase by less than in manufacturing overall.

■ The evidence doesn't support the commonly held view that nationalised industries are much less efficient than those in the private sector. In fact, one of the few comprehensive studies which has been made of their performance suggests that their record in increasing productivity compares rather favourably with that of private enterprise.

■ Increases in the prices of nationalised industry products attract a lot of attention because they are usually announced in a blaze of publicity rather, as with many goods, just being presented to the shopper as a *fait accompli*. Moreover, because we all consume public enterprise goods and services on a large scale, their price changes do have a substantial impact on family budgets. It can, however, be argued that, if anything, the prices charged by nationalised industries during most of the postwar period have been too low rather than too high. Governments time after time have stepped in to prevent or postpone price increases—often with damaging effects on the industries' development. And even if prices were too high, it could hardly be due to the monopoly power of the nationalised industries; most of them face intense competition—the railways versus the private car, coal versus oil, or British steel against foreign steel.

■ Nor has working for a nationalised industry always guaranteed high wages. Often in the past, when wage restraint has been the order of the day, governments have tried to set an example by imposing particularly severe discipline within the public sector itself. At times, public sector incomes have consequently lagged behind—although recent wage bargaining within public enterprises does seem to have become a good deal more effective.

NATIONALISATION? IT'S A WAY OF PAYING THROUGH THE NOSE.

PRICE RESTRAINT

A parliamentary select committee reporting on the British Steel Corporation (1973) wrote:

■ 'prices were held at too low a level and below those obtaining overseas'

■ 'there was buoyant demand from which it was not able fully to benefit because it was not free to fix its prices in accordance with its commercial judgement'

■ 'enforced delays and reductions in the price increases which the Corporation had considered proper will have cost it (up to 1973) between £150 million and £200 million.'

■ 'In the fixing of its prices the Corporation has had to submit to direction from outside on five occasions in less than six years.'

■ 'The benefits to the economy of keeping down steel prices have not been conclusively demonstrated. The savings to industrial consumers may have been used less to hold down prices, than to accede to inflationary increases in wages. On the other hand the harm done to the commercial well-being of the Corporation and the morale of its workers is well demonstrated.'

WAGES Increase in Employment Income per head (1964 = 100).		Private companies	Nationalised industries
	1965	106.7	108.7
	1966	114.6	115.7
	1967	120.2	126.8
	1968	130.7	130.2
	1969	139.9	138.8
	1970	157.9	157.4
	1971	176.6	177.5

NATIONALISATION? IT'S A WAY OF FILLING UP THE WORKERS POCKETS.

But the fact that many popularly held views about the nationalised industries may be misconceived prejudices, that doesn't prove nationalisation has therefore worked. The yardstick for judging *that* depends on what we think nationalisation is supposed to achieve.

The bulk of the nationalisation which has taken place in Britain occurred during the immediately postwar years. For the Labour government of that time, public ownership of a group of major industries was the transition from private enterprise to a mixed economy and perhaps the beginning of more widespread socialisation of industry: industry controlled by the people, run for the people and accountable to them. It was only partly the past failures of their private owners to run them effectively which formed the argument that strategic industries like the railways, coal and electricity were too important in the economy for them to be left in private hands.

GOVERNMENTS HAVE FAILED TO MAKE CLEAR WHAT THEY EXPECT FROM NATIONALISED INDUSTRIES.

But nationalisation is not an end in itself—although it may have seemed so at that time. Having taken an industry into public ownership, then what next? According to what principles should it be run? That's a question to which governments have given different, and often confused, answers—when they have bothered to think about it at all.

To highlight the issue, we'll concentrate on just one of the nationalised industries—the railways. How should they be run? What sort of railway system should we expect from a public enterprise? There are three broad alternatives to choose from.

The first is to tell them to behave just as if they were private enterprises, and to make as large profits as possible. In this case, the only point in having nationalised them would be that the profits go to the nation rather than private shareholders. But what would a profit-maximising railway service look like? It means examining every part of it and finding out whether it pays. If it doesn't and can't be made to do so, then it should be scrapped. That in fact was the exercise that Dr Beeching was recruited from I.C.I. to do in the early sixties.

In his 1963 report *The Reshaping of British Railways,* the doctor concluded that drastic surgery was needed—a halving of the route mileage from 17,000 to 8,000 and the closure of about 700 stations and halts. Many of these cuts have subsequently been made, and if today the railways were to be made into money-makers, the railway network would probably need even more severe pruning than in the Beeching era.

Is *this* the sort of railway service which we want?

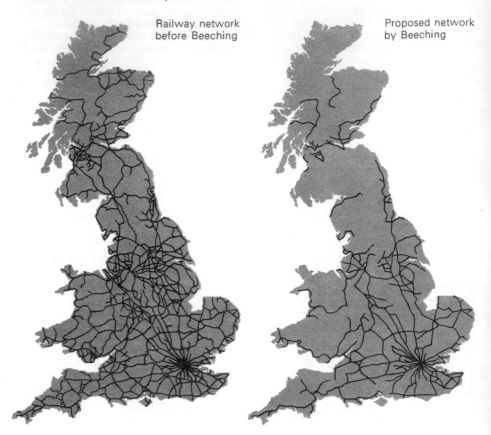

Railway network before Beeching

Proposed network by Beeching

The second alternative is to run the railways as a social service. This would mean keeping lines and services open even when they are known not to pay— when the charges made are insufficient to cover costs. The size of the railway network would then depend on a government decision about the extent of the public service which it thinks ought to be provided. The implication, of course, is that the railways would regularly face an annual shortfall in their finances which would have to be made good out of the general exchequer. However, these shortfalls should not be labelled 'losses', which carries the odour of failure, because they in fact would stem from a conscious policy decision. Government payments to the railways would not be subsidies of their inefficiency so much as contributions by taxpayers analagous to those which we make towards running the National Health Service.

Is *this* the sort of railway service which we want?

The final alternative is for the railways to be run on *economic* lines. This may sound just the same as telling them to behave like private enterprises, but it is not. The popular notion that 'economic' means 'what pays' is true only if payability is measured in terms of the economy as a whole rather than from the viewpoint of a particular enterprise.

When a private company works out its profit, it naturally only looks at those costs and revenues which show up in its own balance sheet. But this is commercial rather than economic accounting. What's left out (and what would be included if an economic criterion were being applied) are both the costs which the activities of the firm inflict on others, and also any resulting benefits which others enjoy but which don't appear in the firm's balance sheet.

The possible divergence between private and social costs and benefits can be considerable. In the case of transport, for example, the effect of closing a railway line extends beyond the saving in cost (and loss of revenue) to the railway itself. On top of that, there is the increased road congestion which results, the loss of local jobs, the wastage of houses and schools if people are forced to move out of an area because of the lack of transport facilities. Running the railways on an economic rather than a narrowly commercial basis means taking these wider costs and benefits into account. In the process, the railways are likely to 'lose money'. But the point that needs to be made clear is that such 'losses' are worth while—because they are more than offset by gains to the economy as a whole.

Is *this* the sort of railway service which we want?

The trouble is that what we seem to expect from the railways is an impossible combination of all these three approaches. A corner seat for every one of us and yet low fares, services at odd hours and to remote places, an extensive and efficient network which pays its own way—*that's* the sort of railway system which we want. And obviously, we can't have it.

And if the distinction between the commercial, social service and economic approaches to running public enterprises has not been clear in the minds of the general public, governments too have been slow in making clear the principles on which, and why, they expect nationalised industries to run.

The sixties did see some progress (in the White Papers of 1961 and 1967) in distinguishing between the commercial activities of nationalised industries for which the government now sets financial targets to be met, and the provision of financially unremunerative services which it thinks are either economically justifiable or socially desirable and for which subsidies are therefore needed.

But the general impression has been allowed to remain that subsidies have been required to prop up public enterprise inefficiency rather than as the result of deliberate policy decisions about what they should be doing. Moreover, governments themselves have worsened the plight of particular enterprises by using the nationalised sector as an instrument for controlling overall spending

---

THE 1961 WHITE PAPER
- put the emphasis on setting financial targets for each nationalised industry, rather than on ways of achieving the targets;
- set the target periods and planning and investment programmes into a five-yearly period;
- proposed that nationalised industries should aim to cover the cost of replacing their investment by their pricing policies, and not just cover the amount it had originally cost them.

THE 1967 WHITE PAPER
- put the emphasis on how financial targets were to be achieved; that is, on pricing and investment policies;
- proposed that the full and true cost of supplying the customer should be charged;
- set a test rate of return figure against which intended investment plans were to be assessed to decide whether to go ahead.

---

and prices in the economy. Time and again, because they are under direct State control, the nationalised industries have found their investment programmes slashed or proposed price increase restrained—and then subsequently been blamed for failing to meet the financial targets laid down for them.

In all this confusion, it is very difficult to judge how far nationalisation has been successful. Inconsistent government policy about the framework within which they should work coupled with lack of public education about their aims and problems is highly damaging to the morale of those who operate our public enterprises—and makes it hardly surprising that they are so vulnerable to popular criticism. And it is against this background that the current debate about further extension of public ownership and control is taking place. That is something which we shall come back to in Chapter 14. But first, problems common to both the public and private sectors of industry—those arising from the growing size of enterprises.

■ The annual sales of General Motors are now greater than the entire national output of the Netherlands.

■ One in every two workers in manufacturing industries in Britain is employed by one of the largest 200 firms.

■ It is estimated that the largest five firms in each industry now account for 75% of the industry's output on average.

Do facts like these alarm you, and make you wonder whether firms are getting too big nowadays? Or do you see this kind of trend as a necessary thing if we are to have cheap mass-produced goods? Also, do you tend to answer questions like these from the point of view of a consumer or a worker?

■ How would you have voted as an inhabitant of Flixborough: to have the destroyed chemical plant rebuilt there or not?

■ How much extra would you be prepared to pay for a stainless steel exhaust pipe on your next car?

These are questions which you yourself have never had to answer personally, but which require decisions from someone somewhere. This chapter sets out to throw light on the reasons why firms have got so much bigger, and on the pro's and con's of mass production.

On a sunny Sunday in the summer of 1925, you could have taken your family for a drive through the quiet country lanes in your shiny new Sunbeam 14/40 saloon for which you had just paid £685 secure in the knowledge that its six brakes represented British skills at their best. Fifty years later, the car in which you embark on a similar family drive will have set you back a great deal more— £2,000. Although the price of cars has trebled, after allowing for general inflation the fact is that cars have become relatively cheaper over the years. And the same is true of a great variety of other goods like televisions, radios, washing machines and refrigerators. We live in an age of mass consumption. No longer is a car a rich man's toy—car ownership is a possibility for the majority of us.

What has made this possible is not simply that we are on average much richer than we were. It is also due to the fact that many goods can be produced much more cheaply when they are produced in large quantities. Mass production enables firms to take advantage of what economists call the *economies of large scale production*. Bigger, in many industries, means cheaper.

Underlying most of the economies of scale is the principle of the division of labour, or specialisation. Indeed, the division of labour is the most important single source of the high level of affluence achieved in modern times. To begin with, it took the primitive form of specialisation by product—the cobbler, the baker, the candlestick maker producing for the rest of the community and allowing them to concentrate on farming. Subsequently, jobs have been subdivided into more and more specialised tasks—to the stage where today most people spend their working lives engaged in only a tiny part of the total productive process.

14/40 h.p. Sunbeam Touring Car £650. Saloon £800. With Four-wheel Brakes (Six brakes in all). £685 and £845.

Is it a sporty coupé, a family saloon or a handy estate?

Economies of scale

The fibre-spinning process of the textile industry today requires the following separate occupations:	blowroom attendant	supervisor
	blowroom baleman	spinner
	cardroom attendant	spinning room doffer
	cardroom tenter	loom overlooker
	carder	sorter
	labourer	jobber

There are two main economic gains to be derived from specialisation.

■ Workers become more efficient by repeating the same process time after time.

■ Once production is broken down into a series of simple stages, it opens up the possibility of mechanising them.

However, as Adam Smith observed two centuries ago 'the division of labour is limited by the extent of the market'. The cobbler, performing all the processes in shoemaking himself, was appropriate for the village market. But when shoemaking is reduced to a series of stages each done by specialist workers using sophisticated machinery, then the output per man which can be produced is enormously increased. The cost of making a pair of shoes will be greatly reduced—but that in turn depends on a large number being sold. In many industries therefore, it is only the largest firms which can push the division of labour to the point at which the maximum reduction in unit costs of production can be achieved.

Specialisation, on the shop floor and in the boardroom, is the basic reason why big companies can produce many goods much more cheaply than their smaller competitors. Economies of scale take a variety of forms.

EXTERNAL ECONOMIES OF SCALE are those which benefit a group of firms when the scale of production increases. They include:
■ better training of workers.
■ better transport and other services
■ better information facilities (trade journals, etc.)
■ the possibility of separating parts of production off into specialist processes.

INTERNAL ECONOMIES OF SCALE are those which occur *within* a firm as its own scale of production increases. They can be classified as follows:

Technical
■ most automated or sophisticated machinery is only efficient when production levels are high: a small printer will not be able to take advantage of computerised typesetting.
■ the larger the machine, the relatively cheaper it becomes to utilise it: the number of maintenance workers and the amount of power required do not rise proportionately.
■ the linking of production processes can lead to further savings in power, transport and so on: motor car manufacturers have their own foundries and press-shops.
■ the division of labour and specialisation of occupations can be taken further.

Marketing
■ bulk-buying at cheaper rates becomes possible.
■ larger orders allow long production runs to standardised requirements and enable machinery and labour to work to capacity.
■ a new product can gain from the established reputation of the manufacturer.
■ large-scale newspaper and TV advertising becomes feasible.
■ a firm can develop its own export sales staff instead of relying on agents.

Managerial
■ the managers of large companies can delegate much more to specialised departmental staff below them; in a small firm the manager may be cost accountant, foreman, personnel director and sales staff all rolled into one.

Financial
■ a large firm can get loans more easily and more cheaply, and can raise money by issuing shares on a wide scale.
■ uncertainty and risks can be reduced in terms of impact on the firm; what to the small firm may be a catastrophe will only be a nuisance to one particular part of the large firm's empire.

Research and Development
■ a large firm can devote more spending to research and product development, as

well as creating a specialised department for this; a secure foothold—and sometimes a considerable lead—can thus be gained in tomorrow's markets.

THE ARITHMETIC OF ECONOMIES OF SCALE

■ *Increased Dimensions*

Where cubic capacity is involved, such as with vessels or tankers, a doubling of the measurements of the structure can lead to much more than a doubling of the capacity. A container 3 feet by 3 feet by 3 feet will hold 27 cubic feet; if each side is doubled to 6 feet, which would require only 4 times the materials, then the capacity increases *eight-fold* to 6 × 6 × 6 = 216 cubic feet. This is a very real and practical economy of scale with bulk ore carriers and oil tankers.

■ *Linked Proportions*

Where the production process has several stages, the size of the overall undertaking can be crucial in deciding whether or not the firm will suffer from under-capacity or over-capacity. If, for example, the first part of the process is best handled by plant which can take 800 tons at a time, and the second stage by plant with a capacity of 500 tons, then the ideal scale of overall operation would be at least 40,000 tons. This is the lowest number that both 800 and 500 will divide into without leaving spare capacity; the firm would ideally have 5 sets of plant for the first stage and 8 for the second. This kind of scale economy is to be found, for example, in the steel industry, where the ideal integrated steelworks matches blast furnace capacity to subsequent processes.

Mass production, based on the combination of these economies of scale, leads in many industries to dramatic cuts in the costs per unit produced. The total costs involved in setting up a modern steel mill or building a supertanker may be enormous. But when they are spread over the greatly increased output which they make possible, the average cost of the final product is greatly reduced.

Economies of large-scale production are one of the main reasons why industrial production in Britain has become increasingly concentrated in the hands of a small number of giant firms. By 1968, for example, 50 firms were accounting for no less than 32% of the net output of the economy.

ECONOMIES OF SCALE IN STEELMAKING AND OIL REFINING

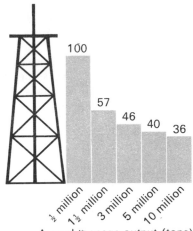

Relative overall production costs per ton of steel: (cost at ¼ million tons output = 100)

128   100   89   79   72   67

10,000   ¼ million   ½ million   1 million   2 million   4 million

Annual output of plant (tons)

Relative operating costs per ton of oil: (cost at ½ million tons output = 100).

100   57   46   40   36

½ million   1½ million   3 million   5 million   10 million

Annual tonnage output (tons)

800   800   800   800   800

Capacity 40,000

500   500   500   500   500   500   500   500

Capacity 40,000

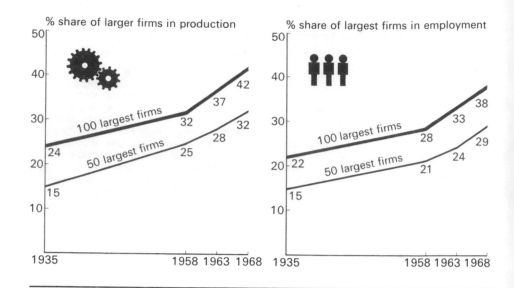

% share of larger firms in production

% share of largest firms in employment

Is big always better?

For the *consumer*, the elimination or swallowing up of so many small companies by the growing monsters has meant a reduction in the variety of goods offered for sale. Economies of scale depend on mass production of standardised products. To that extent, there has been a narrowing of consumer choice over the years. How worrying this is, however, depends on which consumers we are talking about. The rich few may now find it more difficult to satisfy their individual whims than they did 50 years ago. But the mass of people, presented today with only a small number of very similarly modelled cars, surely have more choice than when there were many more manufacturers producing a wide range of models none of which they could afford to buy.

There does not seem much substance either in the argument that mass production has led to a decline in the quality of goods produced. If there has been such a deterioration, it is the result of our demand for cheapness and the consequent cost-consciousness of the manufacturers, rather than of large-scale production as such. We could have better quality—cars with fewer initial faults and ones which didn't rust so quickly—if we were prepared to pay for it.

But for the *worker*, mass production techniques can often mean being condemned to a lifetime of boringly repetitive work at a tempo set by the machine. It is not easy to have any sense of pride or craftsmanship in tasks which have been reduced into simple mechanical routines. And it is not surprising that workers should feel alienated in situations where they are only tiny cogs in the total productive machine.

And there are social dangers in size, too. These may take the form of the greater environmental threats posed, for example, by the possibility of oil loss from a super-tanker or the noise nuisance of supersonic jets. Or they may stem from the fact that the enormous interdependence of the various elements in the economy caused by specialisation pushed to its present degree means that a breakdown or dispute in one small part of the productive process can affect the working of the rest. And finally, there is the more profound problem of how to ensure that giant (and frequently multinational) companies are held socially accountable and prevented from abusing the power which goes along with their size.

Gross National Product of selected countries		Sales of selected multinational companies	
U.K.	36.7		
		General Motors	9.6
Netherlands	9.5		
Belgium	7.7		
Switzerland	6.7		
		Standard Oil	5.9
		Ford	5.9
		Royal Dutch/ Shell	5.9
Denmark	5.1		
Austria	4.5		
		General Electric	3.5
Norway	3.4		
		Chrysler	3.1
Greece	3.0		
		IBM	2.9
		Mobil Oil	2.6
New Zealand	2.4		
		Unilever	2.3
		BP	2.1

(£ thousand million; 1968 figures)

A number of multinational *companies* are responsible for larger sales than several developed European *countries*.

I DON'T EVEN KNOW WHAT I'M PRODUCING.

How *much* bigger is better?

The drive towards larger and still larger companies continues. Sometimes, the growth of the firm is internally generated, with profits being ploughed back to finance further expansion. But more often it takes the form of one massive enterprise either marrying or swallowing up another—as in the frenetic merger and take-over booms of the late sixties and early seventies. Size, we are told, is vital from the point of view of international competitiveness. Only with access to the European market of 200 million people, it is said, can British firms be large enough to compete effectively with their foreign counterparts.

GREATER EFFICENCY IS NOT THE ONLY REASON WHY FIRMS GROW.

Is there then no limit to the size to which firms will or should become. Shall we indeed be in the position suggested by present trends—that by the end of the century 80% of industrial production will be concentrated in the hands of only 100 firms? How should governments view such massive concentration of industrial power?

In Britain, mergers between firms which involve assets of more than £5 million are liable to be scrutinised by the Monopolies Commission. When such a case is referred to the Commission (which is empowered to recommend whether it should be allowed to go ahead or not), the firms concerned nearly always argue that the merger is justified because of the economies of scale which the larger company will be able to exploit. That may be so—if the merger is *horizontal* (one car producer combining with another) or even *vertical* (a car producer absorbing a producer of components). But in many instances, it has been difficult to see what possible economies of scale could arise because mergers have aimed at diversification. Companies have acquired stakes in the production of quite different goods—like a brewer buying a fishing fleet, or a tobacco firm producing potato crisps and other foodstuffs.

Much company growth has taken the form of moving into activities so diverse that there can be little opportunity of technical, marketing or any other economy of scale. From the point of view of the firm, diversification is a way of spreading risks and helping to guarantee its *ongoing permanence*. With their eggs in so many baskets, it is diifficult to see how many of our largest companies could ever be forced out of business by competition or switches in consumer tastes.

In 1957 there were 2,024 UK companies with assets of more than £½ million Their total assets were £9,711 million.

AS A RESULT OF MERGERS:

By 1968 this number of companies was reduced to 1,253. (A reduction of 771 companies, or 38% of the original total) But their total net assets were £20,000 million. (An increase of £10,289 million, or 106% of the original total)

The fact is that economies of scale and achieving cost reductions are only one of many motives why firms try to become larger. The aim of a merger or takeover may rather be one of eliminating competition and establishing a market position which is dominant enough to yield secure as well as high profits. Growth in the size of the company may become an end in itself for the management whose own status is related to it. And for an enterprise to become multinational may be seen as the means of evading the irksome tax and other restrictions imposed by national governments.

Then again, although in certain industries like steel or ship-building, it may be that there are genuine economies to be reaped from further industrial concentration, there is doubt about whether generally there are significant economies of large scale production still to be exploited. Indeed, at least one economist,

E. F. Schumacher, argues that economies of scale have become a 'myth of the twentieth century' in that it is possible to devise alternative technologies through which similar cost levels can be achieved by much smaller industrial enterprises.

Revulsion against mass production techniques must ultimately come from the shop floor. With increasing affluence and education, it will become increasingly difficult to induce people to spend their working lives in monotonous and thoughtless routines. In Sweden already, the car factories are largely manned by immigrant workers as the Swedes themselves have moved out. Producers there are beginning to experiment with smaller-scale, more humanised plants as a possibly more economic mode of production.

It may be, that in many lines of production, such an approach would actually pay. But supposing that it didn't—supposing that smaller scale meant higher costs of production. Then, how far, as consumers, are we prepared to meet the costs of what, as workers, we would find more congenial and satisfying working conditions?

THE MULTINATIONAL DIMENSION
The most recent stage in the trend towards bigger and bigger firms has been the growth of multinational companies—organisations with subsidiaries or associated companies in more than one country. In such cases the advantages are not merely those of economies of scale—though these can be very important. What might some of the other actual and potential advantages for these companies be? And what problems might they pose for governments?

■ Their internal transactions can have really significant effects on the balance of payments of the countries in which they operate. It has been estimated that transactions within multinational companies account for 65% of the USA's exports. The comparable figure for Britain is 25%.

■ By their internal pricing policies they can to some extent choose which countries they will make the bulk of their profits in, and thus minimise the amount of tax they have to pay overall.

■ They can have a big effect on a country's economic position—particularly its investment and balance of payments performance —as a result of their decisions about where they will invest in new plant.

■ They can take advantage of differences and changes in exchange rates in the timing of their internal payments; is it possible that the gnomes of Zurich were British firms rather than Swiss bankers?

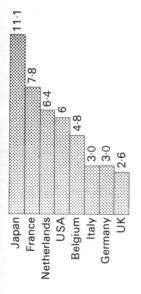

Manufacturing
Investment 1960-73
% Annual Growth

Japan	11·1
France	7·8
Netherlands	6·4
USA	6
Belgium	4·8
Italy	3·0
Germany	3·0
UK	2·6

League tables with Britain in the relegation zone are not attractive illustrations, but they are impossible to run away from. Yet again our performance in a key economic area appears well below that set by our major competitors.

But perhaps there is more to this league table than meets the eye, especially if we think about the relationship between investment and growth: the chicken and the egg.

■ Has our rate of growth been lower than other countries because we have not invested as they have done?

■ Or have we not invested because the rate of growth in Britain has been so low and erratic?

To some extent the choice between these explanations will be a political as well as an economic distinction, and one that is likely to be at the forefront of party politics for some time to come.

In this final chapter we look at alternative diagnoses and widely different suggestions for cures for Britain's economic ills, and we consider whether one of the doctors is one day going to be allowed—and possibly forced—to operate.

In 1972 it was a Conservative government which passed an Industry Act which empowered it to give private industry a transfusion of some £550 million of public money. It was the same government, elected in 1970 on a basically non-interventionist platform, which then nationalised Rolls-Royce and brought in a statutory incomes policy. By the middle of 1975, it was the turn of a Labour government to have deeply involved itself in the affairs of companies as significant to the economy as Burmah Oil and British Leyland—and to introduce its own Industry Bill envisaging still more far-reaching intervention by government in the working of the economy.

When governments formed by parties of supposedly very different views pursue such similar interventionist policies, it suggests that there is something seriously amiss with British industry. And when you look at the general economic scene—soaring prices, rising unemployment, stagnation and persistent balance of payments difficulties—it is easy to paint a picture of fundamental economic crisis which doesn't do justice to the real economic progress which has been made in postwar Britain.

But we are certainly entitled to ask what is going wrong?
■ Is it *governments* which have failed to get the economy right?
■ Or is *private industry* which has failed to deliver the goods?

That is the crux of a debate which is now beginning to take place and seems likely to dominate political discussion in the next few years. Isn't it that governments have taken too much upon themselves and by meddling with the economy have robbed it of its natural drive? If it is, then governments have to learn the lesson that private enterprise can only blossom if it is freed from the stifling effects of State interference. Or is it the case that intervention has been forced upon governments by the need to prop up an ailing private sector which can no longer provide the dynamic efficiency which is claimed for it in the theory of a market economy? If that is so, then the solution will have to lie in more, rather than less, government involvement in the economy.

The main charge to be levelled at British industry in recent years has been its failure to invest in the modern equipment needed to keep it competitive. Governments have tried to induce investment by offering industry various kinds of incentives. But companies have simply not responded.

■ In 1971-1972, monetary policy was relaxed to the point where borrowing became almost unprecedentedly easy. But who took advantage of it? Only a tiny proportion of the easier money found its way into manufacturing industry. The great bulk of it went into property and financial speculation.

■ Bank lending to the property companies rose from around £400 million in early 1971 to £1,000 million in August 1972 and to £1,500 million in May 1973. Over this latter period bank lending to other parts of the financial sector also rose by £700 million.
■ Meanwhile investment in manufacturing industries fell between 1971 and 1973 by one-tenth in real terms.

■ In 1973-1974, successive Budgets offered substantial fiscal incentives to invest more. Despite this, investment fell rather than rose.

'But', answer the industrialists, 'it is all very well making money easily available or trying to tempt us with grants and tax allowances. If we don't think we can make a profit, then there's still no point in our investing. The heart of the matter is this: so long as you go on allowing powerful trade unions to squeeze us as they do, then investment will be unprofitable. And don't forget that profits are the main way in which we finance future investment.'

Here is a key controversy—between management and the unions. Both want more investment, the one to make profits and the other to increase productivity and therefore wages. But they disagree about how to go about it.

■ The industrialist argues that only if wages are first kept in check will the profits be earned to promote new investment (and which would then allow justifiable increases in real wages).

■ The unions say that Britain is already a low-wage economy. High wages not only act as a direct incentive to management to invest in machines but also provide the booming demand needed to generate higher profits.

And so management blames the unions for forcing them into crippling wage settlements. And unions blame management for their failure to provide their workers with the modern tools necessary for efficient production.

From the management viewpoint, inability to restrain wages is only one item in a more sweeping indictment of the role which government has played in the economy. Governments see themselves as having to intervene because private industry has failed. But private industry will say that, to the extent that it has failed, it is *because* of government meddling.

The case of British Leyland serves as a very good example of this. When it became clear in 1974-1975 that very large-scale government support was necessary if the firm was to survive, the Ryder Report made it clear that the company had got things badly wrong and was immediately responsible for its plight as a result of:
■ Inadequacies in top management.
■ Massive underinvestment in the past.
■ Bad industrial relations.

But the motor car industry has for long been arguing that part of their difficulties stem from government stop-go policies, and that in trying to manage the overall level of spending in the economy, governments have unwisely used measures which have discriminated against the car industry.

- Frequent variations in hire purchase deposit and repayment terms.
- Increases in vehicle and petrol taxation:
- Ill-timed expansion of the economy (as in 1972) when lack of domestic capacity forced British consumers to buy foreign cars.

- In the late sixties the National Economic Development Office forecast—to everyone's horror—that imported cars would be taking 15% of U.K. sales by 1975.

- Not only was the 15% figure passed much sooner than 1975, but the actual 1975 figure is turning out to be nearly 40%.

While consumer spending as a whole was fluctuating by less than 10% a year during the late sixties and early seventies, car sales fluctuated during these years by ten times that amount. In other words, governments failed to provide the stable framework in which the industry could plan and go ahead with investment in the confidence that it would be justified.

Where do we go from here?

So who's right—industrialists, trade unions or government? In their different ways, they all are. Ours is a mixed economy, and if there is any common ground between the various factions it might be in agreeing that we have hit upon the wrong mix and suffer from the worst of both worlds.

Belief that this is so is reflected in what seems to be the beginning of a breakdown in consensus politics about the way the economy should be run. For most of the past twenty years, governments of both parties have accepted that they should actively 'manage' the economy, and the difference between them has been about the extent and nature of the intervention which was needed. Recently, however, the older and more fundamental issue has been re-opened—of intervention versus *non*-intervention. It is an argument about whether governments should withdraw to the sidelines and give the market its head or whether the government must assume still further responsibility in the working of the economy. It is the argument between Sir Keith Joseph and Mr Wedgwood Benn.

One way . . .

Restoring the market to its former eminence would involve a massive switch of resources from the public to the private sector. Government, as we have seen, now accounts for something like 50% of total spending and 40% of production in the economy. That spending would have to be slashed, that production largely returned to private hands.

The advocates of a return to the market as the main method of deciding how resources should be used claim three principal merits for it:

- It would put business back under the control of those who understand it— businessmen rather than civil servants or politicians.
- It would give back to individuals responsibilities and freedom of choice which have been consistently usurped over the years.
- It would stop governments printing money to finance their excessive spending —and thereby halt inflation.

It is not denied that the immediate effects of such a major shift in policy would prove a painful, if salutary, experience. The financial discipline of governments cutting back on their spending and limiting the increase in the money supply would be bound to make credit extremely tight. Less efficient firms would be driven to the wall. And so would those foolish enough to concede wage increases which they hadn't the money to pay for—and couldn't recoup from higher prices because governments would no longer be pumping demand into the economy to maintain full employment. A return to the market would mark the end of the era in which governments have assumed responsibility for employment levels. How much unemployment, how many bankruptcies—that would depend on the speed with which it was decided to curb inflation, and also how quickly firms and unions learned to respond sensibly to the new situation.

After the initial purge, private enterprise could then be trusted to get on with the job with its traditional initiative and dynamism. Prices and profits would again serve in their proper roles as indicators of efficiency, with some firms flourishing and others being 'forced out in a vigorously competitive world. Unemployment would be allowed to find its own level rather than being artificially held down by governments. It would depend instead on trade unions. The higher their wage demands, the fewer of their members would be employed.

The role of government, apart from balancing its budget and keeping the increase of the money supply in line with the rate of economic growth, would be to deal with an admitted defect of the market mechanism: with unequal votes to cast in the economic ballot box, the strong and rich fare better than the weak and poor. Government's job is to protect the weak. But even on this social front, spending should be minimised by making sure that only those in need are entitled to State benefits.

This, then, is the theory of the social market economy—offering the benefits of private enterprise without the unacceptable face of capitalism.

From the same starting point that the present private/government mix is not the ideal one are those who draw very different conclusions. For them, private enterprise has had its chance and failed. The results of unbridled individualism and an unrestricted market system have already been made plain in the traumatic experience of the prewar period.

Keynesianism for a time showed the way forward. The lesson was learned that if the excesses of the trade cycle and mass unemployment were to be avoided, then governments had to intervene to make sure that spending in the economy was enough to absorb full employment output. The fundamental defect of the market system was, and still is, its inability to guarantee high levels of employment.

The postwar experience has shown what can be achieved through Keynesianism—and what can't. Jobs have been protected with a fair measure of success. But governments managing the economy on Keynesian lines have not been able to control prices or get the economy onto a consistently expansionary path.

But the answer to the failure of Keynesianism is not therefore to revert to the unregulated market system. It is to ask why it has failed—and then to improve rather than abandon government management of the economy.

The weaknesses of Keynesianism we have already looked at in Chapter 8: the bluntness of the weapons of intervention, the existence of sectors (like private investment and foreign trade) which the government finds difficult to influence, and the emphasis largely on manipulating demand when often the real problem is one of the structure of the economy. The solution is therefore to sharpen the weapons and to exercise more rather than less control.

It is this which underlies the argument for planning agreements. If companies are receiving large sums of public money, then shouldn't they in return be prepared to discuss in detail their future plans about investment, location and overseas transactions with the government? It is this which is the rationale of the National Enterprise Board which is intended to acquire State holdings in the private sector when it is needed to ensure that companies work in a way

. . . or the other ?

107

which fits in with national economic objectives. It is this which points to incomes and prices policies as the only way of reconciling the maintenance of full employment with price stability.

So it's up to you. The trouble is that the signs are that we're not too keen on either alternative. There have been profound changes in society over the past thirty years. Are we any longer prepared to accept a market philosophy which implies greater ruthlessness, greater inequality and the single-minded pursuit of profit? But are we any more ready or willing to see the sphere of government influence extended still further into the fabric of the economy?

Of course, there's always the third way out, and that is to struggle on as we are now—and to complain about the results.

UK MANUFACTURING INVESTMENT AS % OF TOTAL INVESTMENT

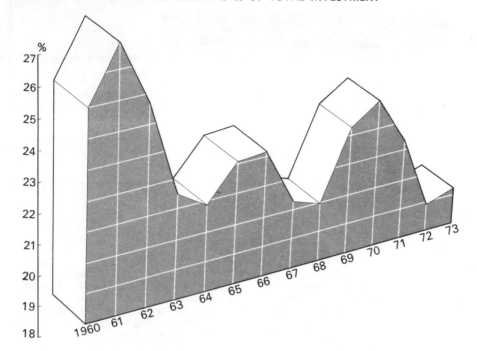

What two points appear to you to emerge from the graph?

■ There is a clear downward trend in the percentage of total investment devoted to manufacturing industries. So not only is U.K. investment less compared with other countries; it is also falling.

■ The fluctuations from year to year display a strongly marked cyclical pattern, giving a good reflection of 'stop-go' policies.

The implication is that more attention needs to be given to the timing and nature of our investment as well as merely to the amount. As a senior civil servant at the Department of Industry remarked:

'The trouble with our manufacturing industries is that if we want a major new plant built to increase the capacity of the industry in question, then we either get none or two.'

In other words, businessmen tend to be collectively over-optimistic or over-pessimistic about prospects. The government's stop-go policies thus become reinforced by industry's own.

One country which has developed a sophisticated set of incentives and controls, involving 'blocked balances' of investment funds which can only be released back to firms when the government judges the economic situation to require more injections of capital spending is Sweden. It might well be a system worth close attention by the U.K., if there is a chance of it helping us to avoid the kind of pattern indicated by the figures below:

Growth of industrial production	(Annual rates)	Overall growth
1955-1958	0%	1.0%
1958-60	9.1%	6.4%
1960-63	0%	1.0%
1963-65	8.3%	6.0%
1965-67	0.4%	1.2%
1967-68	5.6%	3.6%

The figures spell it out only too clearly:

STOP
GO
STOP
GO
STOP
GO

QUESTIONS

Chapter 1

1. Name the four types of costs which can contribute to inflation.

2. Which of these four costs do you think would be *easiest,* and which *most difficult,* for the government to restrain?

3. Which of the following are true?
   (a) the greater the proportion of total costs that are labour costs, the greater the impact that a given wage rise will have;
   (b) a 10% wage rise must lead to a 10% increase in wage costs per unit of output.

4. A firm or industry whose cost structure has a high proportion of capital costs or overheads is called _____ intensive; if the proportion of wage and salary costs is high it is called _____ intensive.

5. Leaving aside the question of any increase in output per employee, in which of the following is the impact of a 25% pay increase likely to be greater?
   (a) electricity supply;
   (b) local authority services.
   What is the basis for your answer?

Chapter 2

1. Money includes both notes and _____ in circulation as well as _____ accounts at banks.

2. Place the following in order of *liquidity* (liquidity is ease of convertibility into cash at a guaranteed value); premium bonds, current accounts, bank notes, deposit accounts.

3. Why have governments allowed the money supply to grow so quickly recently? Is it because:
   (a) more money is needed in a growing economy?
   (b) big bank mergers have taken place recently?
   (c) people today spend more and save less?
   (d) the government's borrowing requirement has increased?

4. An Arab oil sheikh was persuaded, after a lot of effort to overcome his suspicions, to open an account with a major British bank instead of holding all his money under armed guard at home. After a week he became anxious again, and demanded to withdraw his money from his account. At great expense and inconvenience an aircraft had to be specially chartered to fly all the crated banknotes out to the sheikh. When the crates were opened the sheikh saw the crisp new-minted notes and exclaimed: 'This isn't *my* money!'
   What was lacking on the part of the sheikh that is the real mainstay of the British banking system?

5. The proportion of ready cash held by banks as a percentage of total deposits is about:

| 5% | 25% | 50% |

Chapter 3

1. Unemployment is higher:
   (a) in Scotland or the South East?
   (b) in construction or chemicals?

2. Which of the following relationships was summed up by the 'Phillips curve'?
   (a) high wage rises occur in periods of high unemployment;
   (b) the higher the level of unemployment, the lower the rate at which wages increase.

3. Which of the statements in (2) above do you think has been the case *since* 1966-1967?

4. Increases in productivity (output per worker) appear to be linked closely with increases in _____ itself.

5. What are the two types of argument used in favour of a 'dose of unemployment?'

Chapter 4

1 Are any or all of the following necessarily true?
   (a) if prices increase 20% and your wages increase 20%, you are keeping pace with inflation;
   (b) if wages increase 25% and prices rise by 20% you are keeping up with inflation;
   (c) if wages increase 15% and prices increase 20% you are falling behind inflation.
2. Between 1963 and 1974 average gross pay rose 160%, but the real value of take-home pay rose only 14½%. Which of the following account for this difference?
   (a) the tax threshold fell in real terms;
   (b) the tax rate rose;
   (c) national insurance contributions rose;
   (d) inflation wiped out most of the rise in take-home pay.
3. Which groups would be (a) top and (b) bottom of the league table on page 30 if it was re-listed in order of actual level of pay?

4. Taking a high-income family and a low-income family:
   (a) which spends most money on food?
   (b) which spends a greater proportion of its income on food?
   (c) which will be hardest hit by a big leap in food prices?
5. Which description fits each of the following terms: poverty trap; tax hollow; fringe benefit; tax threshold?
   (a) an advantage provided by an employer to an employee in non-cash form;
   (b) an income range where people are under-taxed relative to others on a progressive basis;
   (c) the loss of entitlement to means-tested benefits following a pay rise;
   (d) the level at which a family begins to pay tax.

Chapter 5

1. The real rate of interest becomes negative when the rate of interest is _____ than the rate of _____.
2. Which of the following become larger in the final years that a man contributes to a private pension scheme?
   (a) the amount that he contributes;
   (b) the amount of interest gained.
3. Which of the following types of saving is most likely to be undertaken by
   (a) the small saver;
   (b) the large saver;
Post Office; stocks and shares; national savings?

4. Who saved most in 1973, individuals or private companies?
5. Which of the following are true?
   (a) the level of savings in an economy equals the level of investment;
   (b) the more people save, the more businessmen invest in industry;
   (c) inflation is an advantage to the borrower and a disadvantage to the saver;
   (d) indexed mortgages require the same *real* value of repayment each year;
   (e) index-linked national savings carry no interest, so they can't be a good option.

Chapter 6

1. Our imports can be classified into food, fuel and raw materials on the one hand, and manufactures and semi-manufactures on the other. Which category accounts for the greatest proportion of our imports, and which has been the fastest growing?
2. The visible trade balance is the difference between our exports and imports of _____. The _____ trade balance is the difference between our imports and exports of services, interest, dividends, etc. The combination of these two balances is called the _____ balance.

3. There are two ways a balance of payments deficit can be financed: which of the following are they?
   (a) printing more money;
   (b) borrowing from abroad;
   (c) devaluation;
   (d) running down the reserves.
4. The argument for import controls is that they would reduce our trade _____ and encourage people to buy _____ goods instead of imported ones. The argument against is that consumers would be denied _____ of choice; that our own industries might become more _____; and that other countries might _____.

5. The full advantages of foreign trade can only be realised if three key conditions are met. Which of the following are they?
(a) full employment;
(b) mobility of resources within the country;
(c) people have trust in gold;
(d) some countries have no industrial production;
(e) transport costs between countries are not prohibitive.

Chapter 7

1. Which of the following is true?
(a) Britain is worse off in real terms than twenty years ago;
(b) Britain is better off relative to other countries than she was twenty years ago.
2. Which of the following has increased most since the war?
(a) prices;
(b) national income in money terms;
(c) real income per head.
Which has increased least?
3. Which of the following is true?
(a) Britain has had a lower growth rate since the war than her main competitors;
(b) Britain invests less as a proportion of total income than her main competitors;
(c) Both consumer expenditure and public expenditure have grown less quickly here than in our main competitors' economies;
(d) output per man has increased less here than in our main competitors' economies.
4. If the £ is devalued or floats downwards, what happens to the prices of our imports: do they increase or decrease? Should our exports become more or less competitive?

Chapter 8

1. When total spending exceeds total output, there is an _____ gap. When total output is greater than spending, there is a _____ gap.
2. The Chancellor must get four things right in forecasting the effects of his budget measures on spending. Two are the direction and the suitability or effectiveness of the measures; what are the other two?
3. If the Chancellor raises taxes to reduce demand and thereby inflation in the economy, is there a danger:
(a) that this might reinforce inflation rather than reduce it?
(b) that other policy objectives might suffer?
4. Which of the following are claimed to be weaknesses of Keynesian techniques of economic management?
(a) too much emphasis on demand side, and not enough on supply;
(b) certain key factors, such as private investment and the balance of payments position, have proved to be outside government control;
(c) quality of statistics and forecasting do not allow 'fine tuning' of the economy to be undertaken successfully;
(d) more direct measures, such as incomes policies and planning, are required to deal with the major economic problems.
5. Which of the following are true?
(a) the budget is determined by the government's own revenue needs;
(b) the budget deficit is not the same thing as the government's borrowing requirement.

Chapter 9

1. The value of goods foregone as a result of producing or buying a particular item is known to economists as the _____ cost.
2. Does a demand curve:
(a) slope downwards from left to right, showing that more is bought at lower prices; *or*
(b) slope upwards from left to right, showing that less is bought at lower prices?
3. The responsiveness of demand to a change in price is known as the _____ of demand. If a good has no close substitutes, this responsiveness will be
(a) high or (b) low.
4. Which of the following can limit the free operation of market forces?
(a) consumer ignorance;
(b) advertising;
(c) immobility of resources.
5. If there is an increase in consumer incomes, the demand curve will:
(a) shift to the left?
(b) slope more sharply downwards?
(c) shift to the right?

Chapter 10

1. How is it possible for cigarettes to increase in price and yet still be cheaper relative to other goods a year later?
2. Will a firm's supply curve
    (a) slope up from left to right, showing that more will be produced at higher prices; *or*
    (b) slope down from left to right, showing that less is produced at higher prices?
3. What happens to price if
    (a) demand exceeds supply?
    (b) supply exceeds demand?
4. The supply of food is inelastic, as is the demand. If demand for food increases, or supply reduces, will this have a greater impact (a) on price *or* (b) on supply?
5. How can a Wimbledon tennis ticket fetch £100?

Chapter 11

1. What are the reasons for State provision of goods and services, rather than leaving everything to the private sector?
2. The State is involved in three kinds of economic activity:
    (a) consumption of goods and services;
    (b) investment;
    (c) transfer payments from one section to another.
Into which category do each of the following fall? Building a motorway; providing unemployment benefit from national insurance contributions; running libraries and museums.
3. Are local rates:
    (a) an important source of revenue to local authorities?
    (b) an important source of revenue compared overall to other taxes?
    (c) 'buoyant'—that is, do they tend to rise along with incomes and inflation?
4. Is it possible for income taxes to be a smaller proportion of total income in a country, and yet for that country to be 'under-taxed' relative to others?

Chapter 12

1. How can a nationalised industry have an operating surplus of several million £ and yet show an overall deficit for the year?
2. Which of the following objectives are expressed in the statutes of the nationalised industries?
    (a) they should operate 'in the public interest'
    (b) they should pursue efficiency on commercial lines.
3. How is the distribution of income between customers and the public at large affected if a nationalised industry (a) charges adequate prices and makes a profit; *as opposed to* (b) being subject to price restraint and making a loss?
4. (a) In what sense is the British Steel Corporation a monopoly; and in what sense is it not?
    (b) In what sense is British Rail a monopoly; and in what sense is it not?
5. If the loss of jobs, of adequate transport to jobs, and for some people the total loss of transport facilities is the result of the closure of a rail line and station, then it is possible for the _____ or _____ costs of the closure to be greater than the _____ costs of keeping the line open.

Chapter 13

1. Can you give two examples of *internal* economies of scale?
2. If the first stage of production in a process is most economical when handling 4,000 units a week, and the second stage when handling 9,000 units a week, what is the minimum size that an integrated works should be in the interests of 'linked proportions'?
3. In what sense is a fall in demand for the product likely to be a particularly severe problem for the really large firm?
4. Mergers can be of three kinds: vertical, horizontal or conglomerate. Which category would the following fit into?
    (a) a merger between two tyre-producing factories;
    (b) a merger between a brewery and a poultry farm;
    (c) a merger between a tights producer and a man-made fibre producing company?

ANSWERS

Chapter 1

1. Import costs ; labour costs ; capital costs ; government costs (taxes, etc.).
2. The easiest to restrain are government costs, followed by capital costs. Import costs are the most difficult, as they are largely outside government influence.
3. (a) is true, unless there is a really big increase in output per worker at the same time. (b) is not true.
4. Capital-intensive ; labour-intensive.
5. Local authority services, as this is a very labour-intensive sector ; electricity supply has a low proportion of labour costs.

Chapter 2

1. coin ; current.
2. bank notes, current accounts, deposit accounts ; premium bonds.
3. (a) and (d) are the reasons.
4. *Confidence*: he could not relax without proving to himself that the bank could make all his money available to him on demand. If everyone behaved like the sheikh, the banking system would not be able to cope.
5. 5%.

Chapter 3

1. (a) Scotland ; (b) construction.
2. (b).
3. (a).
4. output.
5. That it can reduce trade union militancy and lower the rate of wage increases ; and that it can reduce the level of demand in the economy and thereby restrain inflation.

Chapter 4

1. None of the statements are always necessarily true :
   (a) will not be true if extra tax payable means that take-home pay fails to rise by 20% ;
   (b) will not be true if the poverty trap operates alongside this extra tax to reduce entitlement to benefits ;
   (c) need not be true if tax changes reduce the amount of tax people pay, or if family and other allowances are raised.
2. All four.
3. (a) top manager ;
   (b) old age pensioner.
4. (a) high-income family ;
   (b) low-income family ;
   (c) low-income family.
5. (a) fringe benefit ;
   (b) tax hollow ;
   (c) poverty trap ;
   (d) tax threshold.

Chapter 5

1. lower ; inflation.
2. both.
3. small saver : Post Office and national savings ; large saver : stocks and shares.
4. private companies.
5. (a) is true : the totals will be the same, although the planned intentions of every- one involved would not have matched originally.
   (b) is not true : investment takes place in property, etc., and can be channelled abroad, as opposed to British industry.
   (c) is true, especially when prices are rising faster than the interest rate.

(d) is true: the money amount increases, but the real value remains the same after allowing for inflation.
(e) is not true: although there is no rate of interest, the savings are protected in line with the cost of living, and therefore grow faster than would be the case with interest.

Chapter 6

1. raw materials, etc., account for the greatest proportion, but manufactures have been growing more quickly.
2. goods and materials; invisible; current.
3. (b) and (d). Printing more money does not enable us to pay for imports when no actual production is there to back it up, and devaluation does not make more finance available for our international payments.
4. deficit; domestic *or* British; freedom; inefficient; retaliate.
5. (a), (b) and (e).

Chapter 7

1. Neither is true.
2. national income in money terms has increased most; real income per head has increased least.
3. All are true.
4. Imports become more expensive; exports, because they are cheaper, should become more competitive.

Chapter 8

1. inflationary; deflationary.
2. the amount of the measure (its impact on spending and revenue) and the timing of the measure (it must not operate too quickly or—much more likely—suffer from undue time lags so as to be of no help by the time its impact is felt).
3. (a) Yes. Increased taxes can raise prices, and trade union pay demands, so that inflation is fuelled rather than reduced.
   (b) Yes again. If the taxes take too much spending power out of the economy, unemployment might result.
4. All.
5. (a) is not true. The government is concerned with the overall balance between spending and output in the economy, and not merely with its own income and expenditure.
   (b) is true. The budget deficit is only one element in the public sector borrowing requirement.

Chapter 9

1. opportunity.
2. (a).
3. elasticity; (b) low.
4. all three.
5. (c) shift to the right.

Chapter 10

1. If other goods go up more than cigarettes, then cigarettes become *relatively* cheaper even though they too have increased in price.
2. (a).
3. (a) price is pulled up higher;
   (b) price falls.
4. (a) on price (see diagram on page 80).
5. Because demand is very high, and the nearer the match the scarcer the tickets; i.e. the more limited the supply.

Chapter 11

1. (i) Where benefits are collective, and cannot be divided between individuals (e.g. defence);
   (ii) Where unfairness would result from the unequal distribution of income (e.g. libraries);
   (iii) Where we think minimum standards for all are essential, and some might suffer if there were complete freedom of choice (e.g. health, education).
   (iv) Where it is impractical always to re-coup costs from users of a service through the market (e.g. roads).
2. building a motorway is (b) investment; unemployment benefit is (c) a transfer payment; running libraries and museums is (a) consumption.
3. (a) yes; (b) no; (c) no.
4. Yes, if other taxes (such as VAT) and national insurance contributions by employees or employers are correspondingly higher.

Chapter 12

1. Because of interest payments on its fixed-interest debt.
2. Both.
3. (a) the customers pay the full cost of being provided with the service, and there is no burden for the taxpayer, even though the latter may be benefiting indirectly.

   (b) the customer is subsidised, and the taxpayer has to meet part of the cost of providing the customer with the service, even though he himself may not be a direct customer.
4. (a) It is a monopoly in the *production* of crude steel in Britain, but it has fierce international competition in *selling* its steel here and abroad.

   (b) It is a monopoly of rail transport, but it has competitiors in road, sea and air transport for both passengers and freight.
5. Economic *or* social ; commercial.

Chapter 13

1. technical ; marketing ; managerial ; financial ; research and development.
2. 36,000 units a week.
3. Because the firm will no longer be able to work to full capacity, and its overheads can no longer be spread over such a large volume of production. This will lead either to a fall in profits or the need to increase prices. In the first case the company's performance deteriorates, and in the second it may lose its competitive edge over other firms.
4. (a) horizontal ;
   (b) conglomerate ;
   (c) vertical.

INDEX